The

Hen House

By: M. E. Nesser

*It has to be difficult to have M.E. as a mom,
so I dedicate this book to my children who have put up with some
embarrassing conversations at the dinner table (and elsewhere).*

*A special thank you to Brian Robbins for his brilliant and
imaginative illustrations which capture the shenanigans that
happen in my wax rooms.*

TABLE OF CONTENTS

1

Love Those Luscious Lady Parts

Pussies are my life. For twenty years I have been making women bald with Popsicle sticks, hot wax, and good old-fashioned elbow grease. I attract women from all over the country who want me to rip off their pubic hair. I am very proud of what I do for a living and have made tens of thousands of women very happy. Not many people can brag about that. So my day consists of bouncing from one pussy to the next amid a lot of storytelling and a whole lot of laughter. And I can honestly say that I am sad when the day is over.

I know not everyone is comfortable with the vernacular that I use to describe the body part in question, but what word would make you feel better? Would you prefer it if I said that I extract pubic hair from women's genitalia all day long? Sorry, that is not happening. My language choice can be a little crude, but ripping out hair from women's crotches all day feels pretty crude sometimes. I have found that my language choice adds to my casual and comical approach and, in turn, makes women laugh and feel more comfortable.

Not only am I an experienced Brazilian wax technician (boy, doesn't that sound grown up?), I am also a storyteller. If you come to me and are nervous or shy, rest assured that I am going to tell you some outrageous story that will make you forget you are naked and writhing in pain. I love to tell stories. I love to make people laugh. I ramble incessantly and talk really fast, but it is all part of my shtick. And the faster I talk, the faster I rip.

My first book was called *The Happy Hoo-Ha*, and I had so many people ask for more stories, I decided I needed to give them what they want. Welcome to *The Happy Hen House*, where *every* cock wants to go.

2

Meet Raunchy Raul

Before I get too involved in the storytelling, I wanted to introduce you to a friend of mine. His name is Raul. He is not exactly a real person that you can see and touch and talk with, but he is someone who talks to me on a fairly regular basis. I think he is really funny, and I love to hear what he has to say. It worries me that someday I will become so old and set in my ways that I will stop using my imagination and will not be able to hear Raul talk anymore. I would hate if the creative part of my brain became dormant. It provides so much joy in my life. I love spontaneous and innovative thought. It keeps me happy and energized. This is probably why I like to write so much because it is such a creative outlet, and I know that I have things to say that will make people laugh. And so I want to hang on to my friend Raul and share his sense of humor with you because he is a really funny part of my personality.

I never had an imaginary friend when I was a child, and now that I have become an adult, I think it is kind of a cool idea. Although I agree that real friends are more important, I think there can be some usefulness in a character that is completely designed from your own brain. Besides, I think an active imagination keeps you young. It can keep your mind active and fun—and I think it is safe to say that we should all try to be a bit more like that. Since I am a fan of children's television characters, I will remind you what Barney the Purple Dinosaur believed: it is good to use your imagination. With that being said, I think there is a little voice that lives in all of us. Sometimes that voice is just hanging out and observing your life. Other times the voice participates in your actions, your thoughts, and your feelings. Frankly, if you let your voice participate in your life, you will find it has a lot to say. I suppose many people ignore their little voices because they are afraid of what they may say. Although most people probably worry about offending others or not being politically correct, I have always been a fan of being honest. I would never want to hurt someone's feelings, but I have never been an advocate of lying to anyone either. It is just not my way. For example, we may think it is okay to tell a friend that her zebra-striped hair looks amazing when, in all honesty, we think it looks ridiculous. I may not tell that person it looks ridiculous, but I would probably say that I preferred it another way. I think most people try to form a barrier between what the voice wants to say and what ends up coming out of their mouths. I guess we can refer to that moment of hesitation or restraint as a filter. And a filter is something I seem to lack.

So it's my opinion that more people should embrace that nagging voice that chants random opinions and thoughts in their heads. In fact I think that voice should not only be acknowledged but also revered and encouraged as well. After all, that voice is coming from some mysterious part of your psyche and probably tells you more about yourself then you could ever figure out from hours of counseling. So for those of you who have met me or have read some of my work in the past, you will not be surprised when I admit that not only can I be honest to a fault, but I have enough to say for a whole room full of people. And it may be a bit disconcerting to think that I also have a voice that speaks to me in addition to my actual voice that rambles nonstop, but it is just how my random brain works. So I am hoping that you like my imaginary friend, because he has almost as much to say as I do.

I think everyone's little voice is different. The voice can be funny, or sarcastic, or sassy, or a little risqué. My voice is all of the above. In fact my voice is actually a dark, Latino, homosexual man named Raul. He will not stop with his head-banging commentary when I am working on my clients. He has something to say about most men and women who come into my rooms. Since the parts I am working with look pretty much the same after awhile, I like to focus on other qualities of a person to make him or her memorable to me. I'm sure most people find it easy to link a face to a name, but you have to remember that I don't spend a lot of time looking at a person's face. So I try to focus on some part of the client that makes him or her endearing or unique. As you will learn in subsequent chapters in this book, I hear some crazy shit about people's lives every day and it is the crazy shit that is easy for me to remember.

But when someone cops an attitude with me or is not as impeccably groomed as I would like, Raul will usually chant some funny and often harsh thoughts in my head. In these circumstances I will always remain professional, but he has a much harder time doing so. He gets very frustrated when my playing field is dirty or bitchy or uncooperative. Basically my little voice has my back. So as we venture through *The Happy Hen House*, do not be surprised that, from time to time, you may hear what Raul has to say. When he is in my head and his words are on these pages, you'll know that he is speaking, because his words will be in *italics*.

3

Position #1: Bird's Nest

There are basically only five positions that I put women in when they are getting a Brazilian. In order to take some of the mystique out of this outrageous service that I do all day, I have decided to let you in on what both the client and yours truly look like during the actual procedure. I know that men and women alike wonder how I position the body so efficiently that I am able to remove all of the pubic and rectal hair in less than ten minutes, so I thought illustrations would be the best way to show you how it is done. Throughout *The Happy Hen House*, you will get a firsthand look at what goes on inside one of our rooms during the actually wax. And I have included true stories with each position to make it more interesting. Some exaggeration of each story has been added for your entertainment, however.

A lot of women come together for their waxes. In fact, it is more common than you would think for women to be in the same room at the same time during the service. Sometimes the clients are related. Often they are not. I actually encourage group waxing because when a woman is really nervous about getting waxed, it can be comforting to have a friend in the room. Besides, it almost always ends up being an even funnier experience when there are more people there. *"Believe*

7

me, not only do women like checking out each other's junk, they love seeing each other in pain."

One day I had two sisters come in together for waxes. When the first sister got on the table, the sister who was hanging out in a nearby chair said, "Watch out, M.E. a bird could fly out of her nest!"

Robbins 2014

4
Crotch Confessions Day One

In *The Happy Hoo-Ha*, I chronicled two working days in my life to give you an idea of what I see and hear all day. It was a very well received chapter called "Crazy Shit People Tell Me." In this book, I thought I would do it again over the course of three days. I have added an extra day, because I had that many more stories that I wanted to share. I also tried to be more descriptive with some of the exchanges so you could better understand the point of the story. When you work in a fast-paced environment with a lot of people all day, the conversations vary from the mundane to the ridiculous. It is my intention to give you an example of how a typical day can be for me. Welcome to "Crotch Confessions."

10:00 a.m.: I am starting my day with a newbie. She was very young and very sweet. First rip, she said a baby swear word and apologized. I assured her that a lot of swearing happens in the wax room and that it was OK to swear. Second rip, she said a little naughtier word and apologized more profusely. That's when I told her that she hadn't said the "number one swear word" said in the wax room yet, so it was all right and she was doing great. When I lifted her leg up for rip number three, she said the mother of all swear words with passion and conviction. "Knew she wouldn't let us down."

11

10:15 a.m.: Most women coming in for a Brazilian for the first time are petrified. I get it. You have to get naked in front of a stranger who is going to put hot wax on your genitalia and then rip it off in the most barbaric manner. So it should not come as a surprise to you that this is not the first time that I had a new client come in who was really nervous. The woman was swearing and wiggling around from the moment she got on the table. She said she had been driving by the salon for a long time and had been working on mustering up the courage to come in. It was her birthday, and this was her present to herself. Since she kept closing her legs, I was having a really hard time completing the service. Raul told me, *"You should just tie her down to the bed with restraints because she is making it impossible for you to do your job."* But I did not take his advice, even though it was a really good idea. Sometimes it is hard not to agree with him, because my job can be very frustrating. Instead I tried to keep her distracted with questions and stories, which is what I always do in situations like this. The client would not stop swearing like a truck driver and using all of her limbs to wrestle with me. In this instance you wonder why she even came to get a Brazilian. *"Not for nothing, but if you voluntarily come to Mark & M.E. then let M.E. do her fucking job".* Stop with all the wrestling moves. I am not Hulk Hogan. Since I have made it my personal goal to finish every single woman who walks into my room, I was determined to give this girl the birthday present she desired. No matter what, she was leaving the salon with a full Brazilian. Amid all the thrashing and interruptions, I was able to finish. The best part of this story is when I asked her how long she had been driving by the salon wanting to come in; she said she had wanted to come in since she was eighteen. Today was her thirtieth birthday.

10:30 a.m.: One of my regular clients came into the room and was really excited about some cooking classes that she had been taking with a famous chef. On this day she described in detail the meal that she was planning for her boyfriend. She described every stage of the meal from the appetizers to the salad to the entree. She had different wines picked out and had the whole dinner carefully planned. After she described each course, I asked her what she had planned for dessert. She freaked out because she had totally forgotten about dessert. This is when I gave her several suggestions on how to decorate her luscious lady parts for the final course. I recommended whipped cream and sprinkles. I also suggested mousse and fresh raspberries. She thought my suggestions were brilliant and knew her boyfriend would be totally receptive to the idea. If you ask me, Dr. Ruth better watch out because Dr. M.E. has some great ideas on how to spice things up in the bedroom. *"Another book perhaps?"*

10:40 a.m.: I will never forget this client, because the last time I had seen her was around the holidays. When she came in, she told me that she wanted the shape of a Christmas tree left on the front of her bikini. She then wanted it bedazzled with rhinestones that would resemble Christmas lights. Doing elaborate shapes and decorations can be really difficult and also take a really long time.*" How can M.E. meet the promise of "The Home of the Ten-Minute Brazilian" when she is decorating crotches like a goddamn Christmas tree?"* I left a triangle shape on the front of her bikini line and told her to go to Michaels and buy some glitter. I know that I should always try to accommodate the client, but give me a break. My goal is to properly trim your tree, not accessorize it. On one hand, I felt bad, but, on the other hand, I do not offer bedazzling and have no desire to start doing it. Sometimes I do have a hard time saying no and my little voice could feel my frustration. *"Stop wasting M.E.'s time and go find one of Santa's helpers and ask him to decorate your freaking tree."*

10:50 a.m.: Another woman who comes to me on a regular basis is paranoid about being sweaty or smelly. She always takes a shower right before she gets in the car to see me, which, by the way, is

13

completely appreciated by yours truly. Since she drives close to an hour to get to our salon, she really worries that her lady parts will develop some kind of odor during the drive. In fact she gets even more self-conscious in the summer. A little paranoia goes a long way in my world. One day she came in with a priceless confession that I absolutely have to share with you. On this particular day she had a skirt on, and it was really hot outside. She told me that her goal was to make the drive without getting hot and sweaty. Not only did she drive with the air conditioning on, but she put her left leg on the dashboard and hiked her skirt up so the air could hit her directly between her legs. She told me that she physically directed the vent so that the cold air would flow between her legs, so it stayed clean and dry prior to her appointment. When she got in the room, the wax would not soften on her skin because her skin was so cold. It was hard to get frustrated when I knew what she had gone through to make sure her parts stayed clean and fresh for me. We just hung out and talked for a few minutes while her skin warmed up. Raul and I both had big shitty grins on our faces because we were so impressed with her dedication to hygiene and to me.

11:00 a.m.: My attitude during your wax often depends on what kind of mood you come in with. If you are in a sassy mood then I am going to give you some sass right back. And if you are grumpy, I will do my best to cheer you up and make you laugh. The next client was in a perfectly fine mood except for the fact that she was really hairy. Not only was her hair long and dense, it was really stubborn. When I come face to face with thick hair, I am grateful that I have continued lifting weights on a regular basis, because I needed a lot of strength with this one. We were chatting away and laughing, and at one point I showed her a strip with a mound of thick and nasty pubic hair on it. She said it looked like a dead animal, which actually is a very common description in the salon. But I decided to be a wise ass

14

and told her it looked more like a Chia pet. There was no way she could not agree with me. Then we both started singing the Chia pet jingle and laughing like crazy. I really do have a lot of fun at my job.

11:10 a.m.: I run downstairs to the first floor of the salon whenever I get the chance. Sometimes I feel like I never see any of the hair clients anymore because I am always upstairs. On this particular morning I was really glad I went down to say hi to the people who were on the first floor getting services done. There was a man who had come to the salon to get a haircut who could not wait to thank me for turning his wife on to Brazilians. He said it had changed their sex life. He told me that she was more confident in bed and much hornier. And he could not wait to tell me how much he loved how soft her pussy was against his face. He proceeded to rub his cheeks with his hands and praise the soft feel of her skin against him now that she did not shave anymore. We love that our service makes so many people happy. *"Who would think that waxing pussies would be such a noble and rewarding profession? Maybe our girl M.E. will get a humanitarian award someday."*

11:15 a.m.: There was a strange odor coming from this client. It is tough bringing certain topics up without causing offense, so I normally do not say anything unless I can be diplomatic about it. I would never want to risk hurting anyone's feelings or pissing anyone off. I wanted to ask if her skin and her lady parts were all good, because it appeared that she had some kind of infection down there. I know I am not a trained or licensed physician, but I am a woman, and I have seen more vaginas than I can even count. So I said something like, "How's everything going down here?" She assured me that she was completely healthy between her legs and that everything was good. The aroma emanating from her lady parts was so pungent that I asked her what she used to clean that area. Subtle, huh? She said her pussy was a self-cleaning oven—it had the ability to clean itself, and no cleansers were necessary. Many women believe that, so there was nothing I could say to the contrary and the topic was changed. I'm not going to lie and say that I wasn't tempted to suggest some kind of hypoallergenic soap (or air freshener), but, at that point in the discussion, I knew I had to keep my mouth shut. My little voice was in overdrive though. *"M.E., I beg of you, please tell her that her self-cleaning oven is broken, and she could really benefit from some extra-strength Easy Off."*

11:30 a.m.: A lot of people think that I am clever with my words and stories, but it is really my clients who bring the humor into the wax rooms. All that my eleven-thirty appointment said when she got on my table was, "Take me to the exotic land of Brazil!" And I did.

11:40 a.m.: Don't be surprised if you learn some random things about me in this book that you may or may not care about. It is just about making the stories more complete and for the reader to get a chance to know me better.

I personally stopped wearing artificial nails a few years ago. One of the reasons was that I had stopped doing nails at the salon, so it was not as important that I wear them to show off my work. In fact, it was about three years ago when I decided to concentrate on waxing and stop doing nails altogether. The second reason I decided to take them off was that I kept stabbing women in the butt and legs when I was waxing them. Inadvertently hurting a person on an area separate from the one in question is usually not good for business. So I decided that it was a better idea to stick with a natural nail at a natural length. Just from casual observation, it seems like artificial nails are not as popular as they were in the 1990s. I actually see a lot more natural-length nails in the salon than ever before. So why would I mention fingernails, you may ask. Because not only did this lady claw me with her fake nails, she drew blood. She was flailing around through the entire service and grabbing any part of my body that

16

she could reach. I knew it was only a matter of time until her talons scratched up some part of my exposed skin. And I was right. The next thing I knew, a part of my forearm was bleeding. Sometimes I seriously feel like I work in a combat zone.

11:50 a.m.: This woman called me and said she was in dire need of an emergency wax. (Believe me, desperate calls like this come in on a regular basis.) And I think you will get a kick out of the circumstances behind this emergency. It appears that this woman finally convinced her man to try the little blue pill. With all of his cardiac health issues and accompanying medications that he was forced to be on, he really needed some kind of assistance getting his member to cooperate during the act of lovemaking. So now that he finally agreed to take the miraculous, sky-colored miracle worker, she wanted to be as pristinely groomed as possible and ready to go. And since it took her months to convince him to try it, she thought the least she could do was get a Brazilian. Once again, I was humbled and flattered to be such an integral part of such a momentous occasion. *"If there's a chance you're getting lucky, we're there for you."*

12:00 p.m.: Things change when you have children. Fortunately I understand many of the changes that can happen to a woman's body after she has had a child. And it probably will not surprise you that I am comfortable talking about those changes, especially since I personally birthed three children of my own. It is not uncommon for me to have serious discussions with my clients about personal issues. Frankly you cannot get more personal than working on a woman's vagina. And since a lot of women are frustrated by the changes that happen to their bodies, I try to be as encouraging and supportive as possible. Since my glass has always been half to three-quarters full (as my youngest likes to say), I like to find the humor in situations whenever possible. In most cases my conversations throughout the day are funny. And when the conversations

17

are serious or sad, I try to end the service on a light note so the client leaves with a smile on her face. I think it makes sense that humor would make the Brazilian process much more bearable. This woman was new to the salon, and she told me that she heard I was really funny. *"No pressure."* She told me that under no circumstances was I allowed to make her laugh. She continued by saying that ever since she had kids, she has to suppress her laughter because she has so little control of her bladder. Basically she said that if she laughed, she would probably pee on me. All I could do was laugh because I completely understand how fragile the bladder can be after a woman has a child. So I was not worried about getting peed on. In fact, it has happened before. *"And we're happy to report that she never pissed on our playing field."*

12:15 p.m.: Women grab me during their waxes on a daily basis. It usually does not bother me unless they grab one of my arms. If you think about how a wax is performed then you will understand that I need both of my arms to rip the hair off properly. This client was loud and extremely animated, and she did more than just grab me. Every time I would pull off a strip, she would sit up and hug me. Each time she would hug a different portion of my torso. It was odd. If I did not get all the wax off in one strip, she would get the wax all over the place. For example, I pulled a strip off her bikini line, and she sat up really quickly. When I laid her back down, the remaining wax from her bikini line was all over her stomach and her leg. It was a mess. As we were finishing, she said that she did not think the two Xanax helped any. Now, if I took two Xanax, I would have been in a comatose state. It obviously did not affect her in that way. In fact, she said she felt so high after taking the medication that her husband had to drive her to the salon. When I finished the service, she told me that she did not think that the drugs helped her tolerate the wax any better. *"No kidding!"*

12:30 p.m.: In my first book, I wrote a long and nasty chapter on hygiene called "What's That Smell?" It went into detail about almost every body part and how each part has the ability to be really unpleasant. When this appointment walked into the room, she confessed that she had read The Happy Hoo-Ha and was paranoid about coming in for a wax after reading the chapter on hygiene. That chapter was very deliberate on my part because of all the unpleasant circumstances I have come across in the past twenty years. My goal was to make people more conscientious when coming in for a service with me or any other technician. This conscientious and beautiful woman told me that she put a breath mint in her mouth because I was going to be waxing her eyebrows as well as performing her Brazilian. She also said that she was tempted to put one in her snatch so that smelled minty fresh as well. Now, that is a woman who read that chapter thoroughly and responded accordingly. Not only did I appreciate her thoughtfulness; I laughed my ass off.

12:40 p.m.: I refer to first-time Brazilian clients as "virgins." Well, they are virgins to me and to the service. And sometimes I refer to the experience as popping their Brazilian cherry. It was actually a client who referred to her first experience with me as that, so I have continued to use that expression because it is appropriate and kind of funny. Remember, a sense of humor is important in this line of work. Another thing to remember is that a vagina has a heightened sense of feeling after a wax. When I popped the Brazilian cherry on this particular client, she cleaned up while I waxed her friend. After she got dressed and sat down to wait for her friend to be finished, she yelled, "My pussy has a heartbeat!" I believe it does.

1:00 p.m.: I love this next woman. She came in and was in a tizzy because her shower hose had broken. She told her husband he had to get a new shower head with a hose immediately because she was planning to come get a wax, and the only way to truly clean your lady parts was to take the hose off and put direct pressure on the area in question. Was I clear enough when I said I loved this client? Because I do.

1:15 p.m.: If you expect to have sex right after your wax, don't be surprised if I tell you that your man must lick your wounds first.

1:30 p.m.: Many men and women who wax have had adverse effects from shaving and are willing to try something that they perceive will be painful and possibly humiliating in hopes of maintaining a happier, hairless body part. And the way some people describe their shaving escapades is absolutely hysterical. This appointment was no exception. The girl told me that shaving was like four-wheeling with a Prius.

1:40 p.m.: I am all about being honest, and I love when people are honest with me. Sometimes honesty can come in the form of criticism, which can be difficult to hear. Sometimes it is heartfelt and gut-wrenching, which can also be difficult to hear. And sometimes it is just plain funny. This woman told me to watch out because she planned to fart on me. It was a little different start to the conversation than "how is your day going?" but I went with it. I mean it was just a matter of fact that she put out there when she hopped up on the table. I wonder if she thought she was the first person to ever fart on me. Honestly, as long as it is not too stinky, I can handle it. It is one of the risks a person takes when he or she is working on that particular part of the body. Some people have gas that can clear a room. That makes it a little harder to complete the service in a thorough manner. But, hey, I have an idea. Don't come in for a wax after eating a burrito supreme at Taco Bell!

1:50 p.m.: Although waxing often hurts during the actual procedure, it is pretty uncommon for the hurt to continue once I have completed the service. This girl was walking funny when she exited the wax room. Women rarely walk any different after their Brazilian than before it, so I was worried something had happened that I was not aware of. I asked her why she was walking that way. She said that even though it did not hurt, she felt that walking with her legs far apart seemed necessary. I'm not sure if she was worried that walking with her legs close together would irritate her skin or if she was concerned that her heightened sense of feeling between her legs would make her cum as she walked down our stairs.

2:00 p.m.: I love to hear that some of my ladies have men who share in their grooming experiences. Men often offer suggestions or expressions that are really comical and deserve to be repeated and shared. This girl's husband was hoping she would take care of her "fur-gina," because it was getting out of control. No problem. I skinned that cat. In fact I have skinned thousands of pussies in my lifetime.

2:15 p.m.: When women compare childbirth to Brazilians, I would like to think that they had a quick and painful experience that was well worth it. This was one of those instances. This appointment told me that childbirth prepared her for a Brazilian. It was definitely worth the pain. And then she thanked me. I still think a baby is a better prize, but bald pussies rock too.

2:20 p.m.: The next person who walked into the salon was someone I had not seen in fifteen years. I used to do her nails back in the days when acrylics were popular, and my hand-painted nail art set me apart from most other salons. When she saw Mark, she commented on how he always reminded her of Antonio Banderas. Although she commented on how he no longer had long, dark hair, she thought that he still looked like him and had aged well. And I agreed with her. It was funny that she didn't recognize me at first because I am no longer blond. At least I was not blond on that particular day. It was not until she heard my voice that she realized who I was. Don't people realize that in this business we change our hair color with the seasons? And sometimes we change it even more often than that. Anyway, I brought her to the wax room and found out that this was her first Brazilian. She was really concerned about whether or not I had ever waxed a black woman before. I assured her that at least one-third of my clientele is black. She thought I was bullshitting her, and it actually took me a while to convince her that in twenty years, she was not the first black woman I was about to wax. She was afraid that her hair would be so much more difficult for me to do. As it turned out, she was easy, and I had her bald in less than five minutes. Hey, we're not called "The Home of the Ten-Minute Brazilian" for nothing!

2:30 p.m.: It is common for women coming in for their first wax to ask strange questions. And I am totally okay with this. It is a bizarre and frightening service, and until you have had it done, you really do not know what to expect. This was another virgin who had a fairly strange question for me. She wanted to know if she could go to work after I finished her Brazilian. The question actually surprised me because no one had ever asked that before. Most people are more concerned with how long they have to wait before they have sex. I assured her that this was not a medical procedure but a fairly simple salon service. I told her that aside from a little redness, heat, and possible tenderness, most women are completely fine when they leave the salon. No one has ever told me that they needed to stay home from work because they were too sore to do their job. I'm sure there are certain professions where going to work right after a wax would not be the smartest idea in the world. Pole dancers, for example, may want to wait to go to work. Grinding their kitty on a pole right after a wax may make said kitty very angry.

2:45 p.m.: You do not have to be sexually active in order to get a Brazilian. Not only do I do legitimate virgins (you know, the kind who have never had sex); I do women all the time who are not currently sexually active. Waxing makes you feel cleaner and better, unlike shaving, which can be very irritating to the skin. As soon as this girl got on the table, she warned me that she had a very sensitive vagina. She told me that her vagina does not see any sun or any action. It was an interesting declaration, but I appreciated her honesty. I promised to be careful with her highly precious and sensitive cargo.

3:00 p.m.: A lot of women like to take care of all of their vagina appointments in one day. This girl was no exception. She told me it was her "cooter" abuse day. She went to her gynecologist, and then she came to me. I would have done it in reverse.

3:10 p.m.: It is always interesting to find out where clients hear about our salon and also about me in particular. Most new people come from referrals, although it has become much more popular for people to find me on the Internet. This particular client heard about me from the Build-A-Bear store. She told me she was at a birthday party with her toddler, and she randomly asked another mom if she had ever had a Brazilian. It totally makes sense to me that she would think about hair in a place full of hairy creatures.

3:20 p.m.: More women in their fifties and sixties are coming to get Brazilians. I love doing a wider age range of clients. It makes my days even more interesting. My older clients, for the most part, are much more comfortable being naked and will say whatever they are thinking. And I love that. And as you grow older, your hair growth tends to slow down, so many of my postmenopausal clients do not need to come as often. This client gave me the nicest compliment. She said she loved coming to the salon because I always have the best stories and it makes the service pass really quickly. She also said that she wished her hair would grow faster so she could come in more often because she really looked forward to seeing me and hearing my stories. I cannot even tell you how flattered I was. It was so much nicer than the hundreds of clients who tell me that they dread coming to see me even though they think it's worth it. *"Or the ones that tell you they hate you for hurting them."* Oh, lighten up. I know it's a love-hate relationship.

3:30 p.m.: Once again I am faced with a new client who had never been waxed. It probably will not surprise you that Brazilian virgins tend to sweat. In fact they are usually sweating before they even get onto the table. This woman was no exception. She was working up her sweat pretty steadily when she said, "I should have gotten my hair done *after* this appointment. Girl, I'm going to sweat this weave right off!" *"It's actually a funny kind of irony that chicks pay to have hair sewn into their heads and also pay to have hair ripped off their crotches."*

3:45 p.m.: The initial feeling of having someone rip off a strip of pubic hair is very shocking, but the traumatic feeling tends to dissipate quite quickly. It really is just like ripping a Band-Aid off a hairy body part. When I finished this wax, the girl actually told me it felt like I punched her vagina. Just for the record, I have never punched anything in my entire life, and I most definitely would never punch a vagina. They are too precious to me. *"Besides, they are helping three of our kids go to college."*

3:50 p.m.: I have a lot of fun with this next client. She is a woman in her sixties who drives a school bus for a living. So she starts talking about the expression "I feel like I've been hit by a bus." She said she now had firsthand experience of what that felt like, and it was way worse than she could have ever imagined. The previous week she had been walking through the area at the school where the buses are parked, and one of her coworkers was driving through the area, did not see her, and actually hit her. She was thrown for over ten feet. Besides feeling really beaten up, she walked away with nothing broken, which was a miracle. So she said if anyone ever says, "I feel like I was hit by a bus," she can tell that person that she really was hit by a bus, and it really fucking hurts. And after that experience, a Brazilian is a piece of cake.

4:00 p.m.: When this girl told me her "Velcro bush" was ruining her pretty panties, I knew that she would be hooked on Brazilians.

4:15 p.m.: People often swear like truck drivers and whine like babies when I am waxing them. And I get it because waxing really is painful for some people. Many like to blame me for their discomfort, which is understandable since I am the one causing them the pain. Regardless of how much anyone pisses and moans about the actual procedure, however, most tend to come back to get it done over and over again. But the following statement made by this client was so clever that I must award her for sharing what has become my favorite expression. This client told me I was giving her a "hoo-ha headache"! *"Maybe we could invent some Bayer for the Bush!"*

4:30 p.m.: I usually only wear a glove on my right hand when I do a Brazilian. If I wear a glove on my left hand, it tends to get stuck to the stick, and then I make a big mess. So I am just very conscientious that I only touch the client's skin with my gloved hand, unless, of course, I see something creepy. Then I get another glove on as quickly as possible. I started waxing this woman when I saw that she had some open red sores on her lips. So I put another glove on nonchalantly and asked her what was going on down there. She said that there was nothing wrong with her pussy, and she was kind of offended that I would have insinuated otherwise. I didn't want to argue with her so I just changed the subject. But I have to ask, how would you feel about playing in a sea of herpes?

4:45 p.m.: Once again I have a female client bring in her gay male best friend to hold her hand. I have several gay men who come into the salon with their female friends. Sometimes I think if the male friend ever had doubts about his sexuality, all he would have to do is see a hairy pussy get tortured by me in a variety of humiliating positions to reassure himself what team he wants to play on. Raul agreed wholeheartedly with me on that one.

5:00 p.m.: This client had never had a wax before but was referred to me by one of her friends. She actually had a very sad story. But I am happy to say that by the time the service was over, we were both laughing quite loudly. She told me that she was married for eighteen years and had never fully consummated her marriage. They tried twice, but his member died upon entry. She wanted him to try counseling and felt bad that he had a problem, but she also felt very frustrated and very alone. Finally, after enduring a sexless marriage for that long, she got the courage to leave him. Now she had a man who wanted her, and she was so much happier. I asked her how the hell she went so long without having sex. She told me it was really hard and that she should have bought stock in Duracell batteries a long time ago because now she would be a very rich woman.

5:15 p.m.: Although my day is winding down, there are still some fun people slated to come into the salon. These two girls drive close to an hour every four weeks to see me, which is why they come at the end of the day. One of the girls recently broke off her engagement and is out there dating again. I asked her how the dating scene was going. She said, "Don't you mean the 'fucking' scene?" So I apologized and asked her how the "fucking" scene was going. It appears to be going well. She makes getting Brazilians a definite priority now.

5:45 p.m.: Sassy women with attitudes are always an added bonus to my day. This woman walked into the room with her hands on her hips and told me that before she took her pants off, I needed to go and get my machete. She was not kidding.

It is Friday evening and time for a cocktail. I was thinking about creating a bar menu for my Brazilian ladies. The following are just

26

a few of my ideas to add to the already creative ones on the market, such as an orgasm, a slippery nipple, and a blow job, to name a few.

Creative Crotch-tails
Vagatini
Not So Fuzzy Navel
Happy Hoohasmo
Slippery Grundle
Pussitini
Crotchmopolitan
Slow Gin Fuck
Penis Colada
Strawberry Dickery
A Manhandler
Tanqueray and Tongue
Black Vulva
Tom Cunnilingus
Dark and Snatchy
Long Island Twat
Mai Tits
Rusty Nipple

5
More Twat Talk Day Two

8:00 a.m.: If you happen to notice from the time on the left, we open earlier on Saturdays. I have two friends come in together promptly at eight. They are both freshly showered and ready to go, which is always a good thing. One woman is a virgin, and the other is a regular customer of Mark & M.E. The virgin insists that she wants to go first, which is what I usually encourage. She takes off her sweats and panties in one quick swoop, looks at them, and realizes that she just got her period. She starts totally freaking out and cannot decide what to do. I see women all day long with their periods, so I really couldn't care less. She is standing there doing this awkward "I just got my period, and I am naked, and I don't know what the fuck to do next" dance. I tell her to shove a paper towel in the entrance to clean it out, and I will wax her quickly before it can really get started. As I am finishing her, I ask the girls what else they had planned for the day. The girl on the table with her period said she was ready for a drink. I suggested that since it was morning, they should go for bloody Marys. Then I started laughing and said, "Get it? Bloody," pointing to her pussy, "and Mary," pointing to myself!

8:20 a.m.: I am excited because this is another new client this morning. Her girlfriend told her to come see me. During the wax I asked her if her friend gave her any advice before coming to the salon.

29

She told me that all she told her was to make sure she wore her hair scarf to the appointment. I had no idea what this meant. She told me that she knew she was going to sweat, and she did not want to get any of her hair color on my pillow. In twenty years, no one has ever said they were wearing a scarf for that reason. I thought it was very considerate of her to be concerned about my linens and also very strange that this was the only advice her friend gave her. *"Honestly, you'd think she'd be more concerned about her hair down below than her hair up above."*

8:30 a.m.: This client walked into the room, and the first thing she did was apologize for being fat. I told her what I tell every woman who is worried about her size. I do not care if you are fat as long as you are clean. And I really mean it. I also told her that I did not consider her fat because when she was lying down on the table, her entire pubic area was visible to me without my having to move any parts out of the way. How I said it to her was more like, "You aren't a big girl. If your vag is in my face, it's all good." She started laughing so hard. She said she had never been told she was not fat because her "vag" was in someone's face. *"It's Gospel, according to Mary Elizabeth."*

8:45 a.m.: I like to be warned when something out of the ordinary is going to be lying on my table. This girl comes in the room and tells me to beware because she has a "vajungle" down there. I thought that was a very clever description of her situation, and I told her not to worry because I am the master of taming wild animals in the jungle.

9:00 a.m.: There are just some services that you should never buy a Groupon for. One of them is a Brazilian. Due to finances, this client went somewhere else to get waxed. She had to buy three waxes for ninety-nine dollars. That does sound like a good deal since the current national average cost is approximately fifty dollars each time. She is a slender lady with normal pubic hair, so it usually takes me about five to six minutes to complete the service. At the salon she went to with her discounted coupon, it took an hour. And there was a lot of hair left behind. She said she never thought it would end. She also could not believe how incredibly painful it was. And to make matters worse, she could not exercise for three days because her skin was so red, inflamed, and irritated. That sounds like quite a deal, doesn't it? She ended up only using one of the three services because she could not imagine going through such a torturous experience again. So, in the end, she did not save any money. In fact, it cost her more. I asked her if she gave the other two Brazilians to anyone else to use. She said she would not even give the coupons to someone she didn't like.

9:10 a.m.: Here comes a bride. Getting a Brazilian is as important as the white dress. But oh, no—she committed a fatal error. She got a spray tan before her wax! Talk about goofy-looking. Lesson number one for any spray tanners out there thinking about getting any body part waxed: wax first then tan. Otherwise you will have some very strange markings on your body. I do not think my bride was going for the white bull's-eye look in the center of her body, but that is exactly what she got. *"Who knows, maybe that will help her new husband find his mark better!"*

9:20 a.m.: Everybody wants a deal. Whether you have a lot of hair or your hair is starting to come in finer and thinner, it takes me roughly the same amount of time and the same amount of wax to do a Brazilian. If your hair is longer or denser, it just takes more strength and finesse on my part to successfully remove it. I am not giving this client a discount because it has only been four weeks, and she thinks she should only have to pay a maintenance price on the Brazilian. Every four weeks is the ideal amount of time between waxes. If your hair is finer and thinner then you should be kissing my feet and praising me as God's gift to hair removal, not complaining

31

about the price. Where else can you get a wax in five minutes? And how many technicians have twenty years' experience? I am not the most expensive place to get waxed in our city, even though I could probably charge more, and I would still be booked solid. I am actually one of the least expensive. Okay, I know I sound a little heated, but I cannot afford to give my services away. It is funny because I actually thought Raul would also chirp in with some attitude, but I did not give him a chance. *"You go girl!"*

9:30 a.m.: Vaginas are not the only body part I wax. I actually still wax every part of the body. My second-most-popular part to wax is the eyebrows. Eyebrow clients are sent to the second floor of the salon, where I do Brazilians, so I do not have to run up and down the stairs all day. A twenty-year client comes into the room. I have waxed her eyebrows forever, and she also gets her nails and hair done with us occasionally. I teased her when she walked in and told her to take her pants off. And she did! She wanted to leave her underwear on because she was only going to let me give her a bikini. I told her that I hated underwear and always got wax on it, so she had to take it off. Okay, that was a little fib. Although I left her with this adorable little landing strip, I gave her a Brazilian. Yes, I am excited. I have been trying to get her to wax it all for as long as I can remember. She could not believe she let me do it. About a half an hour later, I went downstairs, and she was getting a pedicure. I asked her how she was feeling. She told me that she already felt sexier. Yippee! I converted another one.

9:40 a.m.: I have to laugh when women tell me the lengths they go to to make sure their parts are clean for me. I think that hygiene chapter in the last book really freaked some people out. This woman said she uses a hand mirror in the bathroom right before she comes into my room to make sure there is nothing in any of her creases. It is difficult not to get a mental image of her doing just that. And it actually is a great idea that you may want to consider before getting a wax done. I see an awful lot of toilet paper throughout the day. Just a suggestion.

9:45 a.m.: Three women came into the room together for a wax. Two of them were pregnant. We started talking about how cool it would be to have a penis for a day. I think many women would like to know what it feels like to have that awkward appendage hanging from their bodies. One of the pregnant women then commented that she and her pregnant friend currently had penises for the only time in their lives. They were both expecting boys. Clever.

10:10 a.m.: Okay, I yell at people. They yell at me. This client was pissed off that I had gone out of town because she wanted her wax the previous week. I told her that I had two very capable staff members who could have done it, but she was afraid to go to anyone else. She told me that I was like a psychiatrist and that I could not go out of town or hundreds of women would have breakdowns. I told her to start following me on Facebook because I post my vacation time every day for three weeks prior to going anywhere. Although she said she was not a fan of Facebook, she said that she would start doing just that. *"Looking on a site that refers to the face may not seem like the most obvious place to find information about Brazilians, but it's fun to shake things up a bit. Besides, faces and pussies have many things in common. They both have lips. They both like tongues. They both like to be kissed. And they both like to smile."*

This conversation reminded me of a 2003 movie called *Freaky Friday* with Jamie Lee Curtis and Lindsay Lohan as mother and daughter who switch places. Jamie Lee Curtis plays a psychiatrist who was leaving on her honeymoon, and one of her patients was freaking out that he would not be able to get ahold of her while she was away. The next thought I had was about pubic hair. I know it probably surprises you how one random thought could lead me to thinking about my job. But think about this: could you imagine switching places with your mom? Since 60 percent of American women aged eighteen to twenty-four are at times or always completely bald, what would your mother think of when she switched places with you? If she maintained a more natural look and you waxed, I would like to imagine that she would be really fascinated and intrigued with her newfound smoothness. *"Can you imagine the look on her husband's face!"*

10:15 a.m.: I do not ask women to help hold the skin because I do not want their hands in my way. When they do put their hands in the general direction of where I am working, they almost always put them in the wax. I kept asking this client to move her hands away from her lower stomach because she was going to put her fingers in the wax. She said she did not care if she got wax on her hands. She told me that it was comforting to hold on to her fat and did not want to let go. That was a first.

10:30 a.m.: This woman had a sad story, and although I felt really bad about what happened to her, I admired her courage. She was pregnant with her first child when her husband told her that he cheated on her. He also told her that she might want to get tested for a sexually transmitted disease. You see, it was not bad enough that he cheated on her, but the woman he cheated with was a prostitute. She told me that it was beyond humiliating to go to her doctor requesting testing when she was eight months pregnant. Several years later, he repeated his behavior with another prostitute. I am happy to say she has left this worthless bastard and was spared from any nasty things between her legs. He only admitted to his indiscretions with prostitutes, so she does not even know if he cheated on her with anyone else. At this point, it does not matter. He is history. Or as Raul said, *"Hopefully, he is history with herpes."*

10:43 a.m.: I was walking by one of the wax rooms and could hear one of my employees giving someone a Brazilian. There were actually two women in the room for appointments during this time slot. They were laughing hysterically and talking really loudly, so it was not difficult to overhear what they were talking about. I thought I heard the woman getting waxed saying numbers, so I stopped to listen. I could not believe it. She was actually doing multiplication tables as a distraction while my girl was waxing her. The funniest part of it was that she was multiplying really simple numbers and getting the wrong answers. Women will do whatever it takes to get through a wax. Even math.

10:45 a.m.: This Catholic girl was dating two very nice men. One was Jewish. One was not. Ironically, both men traveled to Europe around the same time one summer. During their travels, she was deciding which one she wanted to be with. While they were gone, she spent a very long time designing the Star of David in her pubic hair. When the Jewish guy returned from Europe, they got together, she showed him her creative bikini line, and he figured out that she chose him. When she came in today, she asked me if I could design a heart in her bikini line because it would make her man laugh since she had already done a creative design for him in the past. Since hearts aren't very difficult to design, I was more than happy to help her out. *"She should really thank God that he didn't worship Buddha."*

11:00 a.m.: As previously mentioned, clients will call in desperation for a last-minute wax. In fact pathetic, last-minute people are why my days are so packed. This woman was going camping. She told me that she did not want the bears to mistake her for one of their own. I could never let any client be put in danger, so I got her properly groomed for her camping excursion. I would not have been able to sleep if I had to worry about a bear mauling her in the wilderness.

11:15 a.m.: My summer and winter cars are both yellow. I love yellow. It is a happy color. I do not wear the color yellow because it makes me look jaundiced, but I love to drive a yellow car. Both of my license plates are customized. My winter car says "Mark & ME." My summer car says "Wax It All." So if you pass me on the street, there is a good chance you will recognize that I am the one driving the yellow car. There are not a lot of yellow cars in our city, so I kind of stand out. This client saw me driving on the expressway and took it as a sign that she was overdue to get a wax. And she was.

11:30 a.m.: I have said it in the past, and I will say it again. I am not the funny one. My clients are funny. My job is most definitely funny. I just like to regurgitate the funny things that happen in my life. This girl walked into the room and told me that she couldn't wait to show me her pubic shorts. If that description is unclear to you, please let me explain. Her pubic hair grew so expansive on the front of her bikini area and so far down her legs that it actually resembled dark brown bootie shorts. *"Aren't you glad we cleared that up for you?"*

11:40 a.m.: I love being referred to as "a special errand."

11:50 a.m.: This woman came from out of town to visit her daughter in college and noticed the banner in front of the salon. She told me that her first wax only included the sidewalls, which meant the bikini line, but they called it a Brazilian and actually charged her accordingly. And this so-called "Brazilian" took the same amount of time that it took her daughter to get a pedicure, which meant forever. So when she saw "The Home of the Ten-Minute Brazilian" sign in front of our place, she knew she had to try it. As it turned out, I was way more thorough, and, more importantly, I was able to finish the service in a considerably shorter amount of time. *"From now on, let's leave the detail work to M.E. and the sidewall work to a mechanic."*

12:00 p.m.: This girl said she really wanted to come in for a wax the week before, but she could not because it was "shark week." That was what she and her boyfriend called the very unfortunate week that rears its ugly head every month. At first I wasn't sure what she

36

was talking about, but it didn't take me long to realize she was not talking about the television show. *"I bet he wanted to act like a shark and sink his "teeth" into her after we were finished though."*

12:10 p.m.: I love when people tell me that they have read *The Happy Hoo-ha* to other people. But this was just awkward because she told me she read my book to her grandma.

12:15 p.m.: I also love when women tell me they do not wax for their husbands. They wax for themselves.

12:30 p.m.: Okay, girlfriend, not only do I need both hands to wax properly; I need both elbows. So please let go of my arms.

12:40 p.m.: Some women say the most charming things. This client walked in the room and said, "I am here to get a happy hoo-ha!" Yeah, that's what I am all about.

12:45 p.m.: As I've said, I have made it a personal quest to finish every client who gets on the table. There are only a few circumstances when I will make the decision to not finish. This is one of those instances. Basically I had to tell this girl to stop crying, or I would not finish. I have learned over the years that no one who cries ever comes back a second time. Plus I hate to say it, but crying really bums me out, and it just is not worth it.

1:00 p.m.: I felt a little giddy when this girl told me that my book was a perfect beach read. It is not a coincidence that you never want pubic hair sticking out when you are on the beach. I mean, how happy can your hoo-ha be if it is hairy? So I guess the two really do go hand in hand.

1:10 p.m.: I was very intrigued by this next client. She was a widowed woman who was planning on going on her first date since her husband died. She was feeling very nervous because she had been married for almost thirty years and did not feel as confident about her body as she did when she was younger. She had heard a lot about Brazilian waxing and knew that it was a more common practice today, so she decided to try it. She told me that she was hoping it would give her more confidence because she was feeling so shy about her body. I assured her that it was just the added boost that she needed. Bald is beautiful!

1:20 p.m.: People refer to their pubic hair and their vaginas in the funniest manners. This woman had been plucking the hair across the front of her bikini line but had not touched the hair down below for several months. She referred to this look as her "gnome beard." It was a pretty accurate description. In fact if you look up "gnome beard" online, you will get a good idea of what she looked like. It looked ridiculous.

1:30 p.m.: It is harder to wax someone who naturally has thick, coarse hair. And if they are shaving on a regular basis, the hair can be even more stubborn to wax. This client had been shaving for a while and could not take the razor burn anymore and was frustrated that it was never smooth, so she decided to grow it out so she could get it waxed again. During that awkward growing-out stage that we all hate, she had an intimate encounter with her fiancé. Afterward, he told her that her shit down there really messed up his shit down there. Hilarious! I would love to develop a commercial to promote waxing by using what he said because I think his sentiment is brilliant.

1:45 p.m.: Men ask women the most bizarre questions about the whole Brazilian experience. This client's man wanted to know if I touched her where she pooped and peed. It is a pretty vulgar question, but the answer is affirmative. I indeed touch you in the vicinity of where you experience both of those bodily functions—although I would appreciate not coming face to face with any debris from either of them.

2:00 p.m.: Whenever something new happens in the wax room, I get pretty excited. Today was a major highlight for me. A thirty-nine-weeks pregnant woman came in for her prebaby Brazilian.

She was expecting her second child and was already two centimeters dilated. Her first child came out in less than five hours, so they expected her second one to come fairly quickly. As soon as she got on the table, she told me that she felt something wet between her legs. I took a peek down below and noticed a large glob of gunk between her legs. I know that my description is strange, but it is truly the best way I can describe what was at the entrance of her vagina. I got some baby wipes and had her clean it up so we could finish the wax. It was pretty obvious that this glob of gunk was her mucous plug, and she was one step closer to having this baby.

I did not give her any chance of being embarrassed because passing the mucous plug just means the baby is getting ready to come. I was thrilled for her. I started talking to her belly, giving him permission to come out. I also assured her that if her water broke, I would be very excited. I couldn't care less if it made any mess. In fact I have become an expert at removing carpets (human ones, that is). Her water breaking on the floor, however, would have been a great excuse for me to learn how to remove another kind of carpet in the wax room. Besides, I never even saw my own water break, so I thought it would be pretty cool to see hers. I also told her that my husband had always wanted to deliver a baby, so if her water did indeed break, I would intercom Mark first to let him know so that he could come upstairs to help. Then I promised to call 911 shortly thereafter.

Sadly, her water did not break on the table. I was glad she passed her mucous plug in front of me, however, so I could use it as a learning tool for my staff. The other two women who wax at our salon do not have any children, so they had never even heard of the mucous plug. I explained what it was and told them how I handled the situation. I also told them that it was imperative that I finish the service because she was on her way to having a baby, and this was the last chance she would have to be waxed.

2:15 p.m.: Two girls came into the room together. One was a bride who had never been waxed before. Her fiancé was really worried that I was going to "jack up" her vagina. Her girlfriend assured her that I had a lot of experience and would not do anything to injure her vagina and make it so that she could not use it on her wedding night. I am happy to say that I did not "jack up" her vagina. If anything, I made it look more like a happy "Jill" than she has ever had.

2:20 p.m.: I love to hear what clients tell others about their waxing experiences. This girl told me that when she left the salon after her first wax, she called her best friend, who told her to come to me, and told her that she could not feel her vagina. Happily, she got her feeling back. And more.

2:30 p.m.: This client told me that getting her vagina waxed made it feel hot, in more ways than one. Yeah, baby!

2:40 p.m.: Raul asked, *"Why the hell are black women so obsessed with screaming for Jesus during their waxing?"* I have always wondered the same thing. It really seems to be a recurrent theme at Mark & M.E. This woman was no exception. She was calling for Jesus like she was at church. And that was not all. She told me about a dance class she would be taking at church that day. Her physical reactions to each one of my rips were very theatrical and embellished. *"How about obnoxious, M.E.?"* She was making motions with her arms that resembled the motions people would use during a gospel service when they were praising their Lord and Savior. I just was not sure if her arm gestures were praising God or exorcising demons. *"I think a little of both."*

2:50 p.m.: I like new clients to grow out their shaved pubic hair for at least two weeks before getting their first Brazilians. This lady walked into my room and told me that she had been listening to the '70s station on Sirius to get prepared for her appointment with me since she had to grow out her '70s bush. I love it when someone

40

prepares herself not only physically for her appointment with me but mentally as well. She must have been a Girl Scout.

3:00 p.m.: This girl kept asking me to wait and give her a minute. I do not like stopping. I like pushing on and getting it over with. She even sat up a few times to look at how much I had finished, which I think was a ploy to prolong the service and waste more time. *"Go on," Raul said. "I dare you to tell her to lie the fuck down!"* She was trying several stalling techniques, and I have to admit that I was getting frustrated. Finally I looked at her and told her with a great deal of authority to go to her happy place. She told me that I kept taking her happy place away. Touché.

3:10 p.m.: There are different things that bother women about having hair. Some women cannot stand how hot and sweaty they feel. Some are embarrassed when their pubic hair sticks out of their underwear. Others cannot stand how itchy the hair can be. But this woman actually had a new one for me. She told me that she knew her hair was too long when she had to keep adjusting her underwear. I am still pondering this one.

3:15 p.m.: Women often experience guilt when they go to another salon, stop coming for a while, get laser hair removal, or start using a trimmer or a razor. What is so adorable is that they share their guilt with me and, in a way, ask for my forgiveness. I guess this is where my Catholic name of Mary Elizabeth enters into the equation. But I do not get upset about any of the above circumstances. I understand there are other hair removal options. I know that waxing can be expensive, and people like to use coupons whenever necessary. All I can do is give the best possible service to each and every client, and if someone does not continue to come to our salon, I have to be comfortable knowing that I did my best when I did work on him or her. So I had to laugh when a girl came into the room and told me that she cheated on me after a loyal two years of coming to Mark &

41

M.E. When I asked her with whom she cheated on me, she said a razor. And it was a bad affair that she regretted horribly. She swore she would remain loyal to me always and forever. By the way, that is my wedding song. The original version by Heatwave, in case you wondered.

3:30 p.m.: I ask every new client how he or she finds me because it is important as a business owner to find out where new people are coming from. A girl said that the doctor she works with told her about me. So I asked her how the subject of Brazilians even came up. It appears that the doctor, who is a pathologist, and this girl, who is a pathology technician, were doing an autopsy on a body. The body in question must have had a pretty big bush because the next thing you know, they were talking about waxing. A few weeks later I had a pathology resident come in for a wax. She had overheard the pathologist making an appointment for a wax with me and asked her what salon she went to. The deceased are even bringing in new clients. How ironically wonderful is that? *"Even dead beavers can generate revenue."*

3:45 p.m.: Before I started doing Brazilians, I had an extremely large eyebrow-waxing clientele. I still do a lot of brow waxing every day, but not as many as I used to because Brazilians have become so popular. Besides, the stories do not tend to be as funny when I wax someone's puss as they are when I wax someone's pussy. Here is an exception. This client has thick and shapeless eyebrows and was in desperate need of a good brow wax. When I finished her brows and showed her the mirror, she said she was so happy because she could now show emotion again. You have to love the power of waxing. *"Every puss needs good primping."*

4:00 p.m.: Honestly, I love when clients go to other salons to get waxed because I hear the craziest stores about how other technicians are performing Brazilians. This client went to Florida for more than

42

a month to help out her daughter who had had a baby. The technician was working very slowly, and my client was getting extremely anxious. She told the girl about how differently I did Brazilians and how fast I worked. She also told her how I had written a book that was on Amazon. She suggested that the girl buy a copy. After thirty-five minutes, my client told the girl to stop because she could not take any more. The girl only waxed the front of her pubis during that time. She never did any of the labia or rectal area. The salon charged eighty-five dollars for that torture. The woman did not want to pay because the service not only sucked, but the girl did not finish. She said it was the first time in her life that her daughter offered to pay for something, and she actually let her. She could not believe that was the place her daughter liked to go and promised that the next time her daughter was in town, she would bring her to see me.

After she told me about the experience, she said that she aged that day in Florida. She said that the wax was so incredibly painful that she could not believe it and was still upset by the whole experience. The best part of this story is that she continued by saying that getting a Brazilian should not be like chemotherapy or getting a tummy tuck. It should be a quick and easy service. And when it is over, she should be able to go about her day. She told me that after you get a wax, you should be able to leave the salon, forget about the wax, and go home and do some laundry. Random but quite profound.

4:15 p.m.: I went downstairs to help this client because she had just gotten her hair cut by Mark, and she needed her eyebrows waxed. The last time she was at the salon, she bought my first book for herself and a group of her friends. The group was going away to a cabin for a weekend of drinking and laughing. I am proud to say my book was a major source of their amusement that weekend. They all sat around reading the book, and I have to admit that the stories get funnier when alcohol is added to the equation. One woman started referring to things as "hoo-havia," like it was a place where people wanted to go or be a part of. Even after the weekend, our client said that numerous texts went back and forth saying "our hoo-havia rocked" and how much fun they had at hoo-havia. I was so flattered to be a part of their weekend, and I hope that one day they will take this book on another one of their adventures.

Since I spoke with this client, I have to say that my mind has been racing about creating a place called Hoo-Havia, where outrageous and erotic things take place. I have been thinking about creating a series of short stories about the exotic women who live in Hoo-Havia. I want to thank her for sharing that part of her story because this could be the start of my next project.

4:30 p.m.: Time to go back upstairs. This woman started out apologizing to me because it had been so long since I had seen her. It is pretty common for women to go longer between waxes in the fall, so I just know that I have to pull a little harder and that it will hurt a little more for them. Anyway, she told me that her fiancé said it was time for me to get rid of the tarantula between her legs. I can honestly say that I have never heard anyone refer to it as that before. When I pulled the first strip, I showed it to her and said that I had just removed one of the tarantula's legs. It was so funny. I actually dismembered the spider one leg at a time. Unfortunately, one of the sections was so long and dense that the hair got jammed, and I had to let go abruptly and set up to rip it a second time. That is when I told her that the tarantula bit me. It was one of the funniest wax sessions that I have had in a long time. So I want to take my hat off to the clever fiancé and his hysterical analogy. *"Another career possibility, exterminator extraordinaire."*

4:45 p.m.: The next girl had also been growing her hair for several months. It was very long and dense, but I was up to the challenge. She wanted me to leave a landing strip in front. I had really

44

good intentions to do just that, except her hair was so long in the middle that it was getting tangled in the wax. So the landing strip became very small because I took off way more than I had planned. In fact, by the time I evened it off and made sure it was symmetrical, it was in the shape of a little square. When I leave a little square right above the hood, I have to admit that it looks like Hitler's mustache. So I said to her, "I am sorry, but I left you with a little Hitler." That's when she sat up and said, "Heil, Sassysnatch!"

6
Beaver Babble Day Three

1 0:00 a.m.: It's Tuesday morning and I am rested from the weekend and ready to rip! I have to admit that it is so much easier to wax women in the summertime. Sundresses, sandals, and optional underwear are usually the extent of the clothing that I need to work around. But in the winter I am faced with boots and tights and layers after layers of clothing that seem to take forever to remove. So I started this day with a woman who took off her panties, lifted up her dress, and left her high-heeled boots on. When she lifted her left leg up, I was certain that her heel was going to puncture my ear or render me without sight in my right eye. I kept reminding her to keep her heel as far away from my head as possible. It grazed my hair a few times, but my face remained intact. It was a pretty stressful way to start my day. But it was also a pretty successful way to start my day since no blood was shed, and I can still hear and see.

10:15 a.m.: "I am here to get a happy hoo-ha," said this adorable early riser. And that is exactly what she got.

10:20 a.m.: When I hear a compliment more than once, I get excited. Once again, this woman said that my first book was a great beach read. I already talked about a girl who said the same thing last week, but since I have heard it so many times, I thought I would tell you why it gets me so pumped. Anything related to the beach

47

makes me very happy. My parents had a cottage on the beach south of Buffalo, New York, and that was where I spent my summers. They also had a condo in the Florida Keys, where I spent school vacations for as long as I can remember, and I still spend a lot of time in Florida. I love the beach. I love the ocean. I love sunshine. For my forty-eighth birthday, I had three palm trees tattooed on me to symbolize my three children. There is something about palm trees that brings me a great deal of joy. One day I want to live in a state that has palm trees. So if you tell me that *The Happy Hoo-Ha* is a great beach read, I take it as a huge compliment.

10:30 a.m.: If you have not noticed by now, I am a very enthusiastic woman. Another thing that gets me excited is when women share their marriage proposals with me. And this is no exception. This client lives in a house with her boyfriend. One of the things they like to do is work in the garden together. One day they were outside in the garden, and when she was digging an area to plant something, she hit something hard in the dirt. She reached in and pulled it out. It was a box. Inside was a ring. And there he was, kneeling in the dirt, asking her to marry him. This was the first garden proposal I had ever heard of. I thought it was clever and romantic, and I was excited to share it with you.

10:45 a.m.: This girl traveled over an hour to see me. When I asked her how the ride was, she said that the roads were slippery. After I finished the wax and she was oiling herself up during our cleanup ritual, she told me that she was happy. She said that not only are the roads slippery, now other things are slippery as well.

10:50 a.m.: For some women, getting their periods is a messy and painful event. There is no way they would be able to come in for a wax during that time of the month. Not only did this client have to wait until it was completely over before she came in for a wax, but she gave me an example of how heavy her periods actually were. She said that she tried having sex while she had her period, and it looked like a crime scene. I could hear Raul loud and clear, *"Dear God, M.E. TMI!"*

11:00 a.m.: Some women have no problems shaving, and others experience all sorts of complications. This girl was trying to save money and started shaving again. The first couple of times she shaved were pretty good, but then she developed a lot of strange bumps all over her bikini area. So she went to the doctor because she was afraid that she had contracted something. The doctor told her that she just had a bad case of ingrown hairs. So now she is back to waxing again, and she said she was so thankful she did not have herpes on her hooha. *"That makes two of us darling."*

11:15 a.m.: A lot of women ask me for all kinds of advice, and I am happy to give it whenever possible. Sometimes I like to refer to myself as "Dr. M.E." Ever since this woman had a gynecological procedure, she was experiencing extreme vaginal dryness and said that intercourse was really painful because the area was so dry. We discussed different types of sexual lubricants, and I encouraged her not to have sex when the area was so dry because it could not only cause tears and continued pain after it is over, but it makes the wax process more painful and irritating as well. The best part of the story is when she was trying to describe how incredibly dry her body was. She said that it felt like she had cottonmouth in her crotch. *"It's hard not to get the image of a pussy puffing on a joint out of my head."*

11:30 a.m.: Getting pregnant seems to be much more difficult these days. I have so many women who do a variety of fertility treatments and take a boatful of really strong drugs in order to enjoy the extreme nausea and breast tenderness that accompany the development of a fetus in the body. Even the rates of miscarriages seem to be on the rise, and I feel comfortable making this observation from just the small population that I work with. The next client had difficulty not only getting pregnant but also staying that way. She miscarried several times and was getting very discouraged. The doctors could not find any medical reasons why she was not able to get pregnant without fertility assistance or why she miscarried. She was young and healthy, and all the tests performed on her and her husband showed no abnormalities. After the third or fourth miscarriage, she decided to focus on her diet and her mental wellbeing. She did some research and decided to go gluten-free. Not only did she get pregnant on her own; she was able to carry the baby to term. *"Maybe it isn't such a great idea to eat your Wheaties every morning. In fact, we can think of much better things to eat."*

11:40 a.m.: When you see as many naked women as I do, you get to see all of their surgical scars. This client had a lot of excess skin on her stomach from being overweight and having several children. So she had the surgery to remove her abdominal fat and some liposuction as well. Although the scar from this surgery is from one hip to the other, most of the women I have met are thrilled to have the skin removed and could not care less about the scar. Not only did she have over six pounds of skin removed; they also removed over a gallon and a half of fat. I found the whole procedure fascinating. But there was one part of the procedure that I did not find fascinating. Due to all of the excess fat on her lower stomach, it was difficult to access the area right under the hood of her vagina prior to the surgery. She would often hold the skin back so I could wax her more thoroughly. It was almost as if the top part of her vagina was hiding under the weight of her skin. When the surgeon reconfigured her stomach, he had to move her belly button and pull the skin that hung over the pubic area up to reconnect where the incision came together. This is where things really changed for me (like I had anything to do with it, or my opinion matters at all). When they pulled the lower skin up so it did not hang over her vagina anymore, it forced all of her inner parts

50

to jut out. So now instead of her inner lips, clitoris, and hood hiding from me, they protrude out of her body and are seriously in my face! Being the diplomatic kind of person that I am who lost her filter years ago, I asked, "What the fuck happened to your vagina?" She started laughing hysterically at my frankness, told me she loved my honesty, and explained how he pulled some skin up, some skin down, and then cut off an entire midsection. I might not have reacted so bluntly had I not been waxing her for over ten years, but it was incredible how different her vagina looked. I actually felt like her clitoris was staring at me. It was pretty eerie. But then something occurred to me. If her parts were more exposed to the world then she must have more feeling down there. And she said I was absolutely right. All of her feelings were heightened. The beauty of science and medicine never ceases to amaze me.

11:50 a.m.: It is actually 11:58. This client is running late for her appointment, but she is a regular, and I know that I can get her finished in a timely fashion. But when she gets on the table, she asks me about my opinion on waxing the arms. I told her that I have been waxing my arms for years and that I loved how it felt and how it looked. She said she had been embarrassed by her arm hair all of her life. I would be lying if I said that I had never noticed her arm hair before. In fact I had wanted to wax them for as long as I had known her. She said she bleached her hair for a while, but then she developed an allergy to the bleach. She also said she shaved them for a long time, but she got too much irritation and ingrown hairs from shaving and was forced to stop. Now she was doing nothing but wearing long-sleeved shirts because she was so embarrassed by how long and dark the hair was. So I got excited about the prospect of waxing her arms because I knew she would absolutely love it. Although I was now officially behind schedule, I could not let this opportunity go. So I waxed her arms, and we were both very excited.

The next day I got an email from her. She was totally pissed off because her husband had not even noticed that her arms were hairless. This was the one part of her body that made her self-conscious, and he was completely oblivious to the change. She obsessed over her arm hair, and her idiot husband had not said a thing.

After two days had passed, he still had not said anything. So she stuck her arms in his face and asked if he noticed anything different. This was the only way she was going to get him to notice. Much to her dismay, he said he had not noticed. I think it is ironic how we, as women, obsess about things that our men couldn't care less about. *"He was probably so happy with her hair-free hoo-ha that the last thing he was going to notice was her arm hair. In fact, I can't imagine many dudes really care about the hair on their woman's arms. Hair on the pussy? Yes. Hair on the arms? Not so much"*

This reminds me of a similar story I would like to share with you. After years of going to Florida, spending summers on Lake Erie, swimming outdoors, using indoor tanning beds, driving in convertibles, and lying in the sun, I have a ton of sun damage on my face. It is probably the part of my body that I am most self-conscious of. So one weekend while my husband and son were away at a soccer tournament, I went to my plastic surgeon's office and spent close to nine hundred dollars on Botox for the upper part of my face. Two days after I got it done, the boys came home, and we went to Florida for Easter break. It usually takes between one and two weeks for the face to harden, so it was not obvious that I had anything done right away. After a few days in Florida, I noticed that I could only lift part of my eyebrows, and it looked absolutely ridiculous. Neither one of the guys seemed to notice, so I did not say anything. After a week I was watching the sunset with my son on the fishing dock, and he kept looking at me funny. Finally I had to say something. I asked him if I looked different. He politely said yes. I told him that I was waiting for Mark to notice and that I had gone for Botox. I told him not to feel bad because I agreed that my face looked really strange. He agreed with me in the most delicate way and asked if it would get better. I told him that I probably would have to go back and have a little more done so I did not look so evil when only the far corners of my brows lifted up.

After ten days of getting the Botox done, it was time to leave Florida. Mark and I were standing on the deck, looking at the water, when I asked him if he really never looked at me closely or if he did not want to say anything because I looked so weird. He looked at me quizzically and said, "What the fuck are you talking about?" I lifted up my bangs, took off my sunglasses, and told him that I had almost a thousand dollars' worth of Botox and that he did not even notice! I told him that Zach noticed, but he did not want to say anything because he thought my face looked strange. So now my husband was staring at my face and shaking his head like he did not really see anything different. I tried lifting my brows, and only the outer corners moved. So he shrugged, and that was that.

So there I was, self-conscious about how much my face had aged, and my husband of nearly thirty years really didn't notice or care. I'm glad I tried the Botox because I always wondered if it would make my face look better and make me feel better, but it really didn't. The only way I think I would do it again is if I convinced myself that looking like Jack Nicholson when he played the Joker would make me feel prettier.

12:10 p.m.: This woman usually brings her three-year-old in with her when she gets a wax. Her daughter really likes our dog, Bandit, and she also knows that we have suckers at the salon. Dogs and candy are always a huge draw for children. As they were leaving their house to come to Mark & M.E., the daughter told the daddy that she and Mommy were going to get their tushies waxed. After I finished the mom, the little girl hopped up onto my table on her belly and said, "Mommy, I am going to get my tushy waxed now!"

12:15 p.m.: A big, bald guy came in for a back and buttocks wax. He had never been waxed before, but he was meeting his out-of-town girlfriend for the weekend, and she had mentioned that she did not like his hair. So this was going to be his present to her. He was surprised that the wax did not hurt. He said he had been nervous all week because of the scene from *The Forty-Year-Old Virgin*. I told him that many men have been scared away from waxing because of that scene. I finished his backside then did his shoulders. I also suggested he use a clipper on the rest of his body because, even though his hair was not that dense, it was long and would look better if it was trimmed. When he stood up and looked in the mirror, he could not believe how much nicer he looked without so much body hair. He admitted to being embarrassed by how long the shoulder and chest hair had gotten, and he loved how it looked with no hair on his shoulders anymore. He was also excited about trimming down his chest hair because he did not like how it looked when it stuck out of his shirts. Apparently someone told him he should never trim his body hair. That was silly. If he only wore high-collared shirts so his hair did not stick out then, in my opinion, he needed to trim his chest hair. The best part of this appointment was when he put his t-shirt back on. If you have had back hair for twenty years and suddenly were bald, you can only imagine how strange an undershirt would feel. He looked so incredibly happy. This was probably my favorite appointment of the day.

12:30 p.m.: This was a woman who had tried to get Brazilians at other salons, but no one had ever made her completely bald. I had her bald pretty quickly, and she kept telling me how good I was. (Good for the ego, I must admit.) When she went to cash out, she asked if she could be frank and tell me something. Obviously she had never been to Mark & M.E. before, or she would not have asked permission to speak freely. She said that she had not seen her vagina since she was a little girl and really did not remember what it looked like. So after I had left the room so she could clean up, she told me that she stood in front of the mirror for a really long time looking at her vagina from every possible angle. *"If she plays her cards right, hopefully her man will examine it from every angle as well."*

12:45 p.m.: It is funny what provokes women to come see me. My next appointment's husband wanted to know if she was going for the natural look. She complained that she was busy and would make the appointment as soon as she got a chance. Fortunately, today was that chance. So then he wanted to know why she did not shave that area. She told him that shaving was no longer an option. That makes me proud. What bothers me about this conversation is the expression "the natural look." Although I understand that natural refers to the way God intended, I still have issues with it. If being hairy is natural, does that mean that the millions of women who have no pubic or body hair are "unnatural"? And what about underarm hair? Is growing the hair on that part of the body supposed to be better, because it is deemed "natural?" *"I think women who grow their upper lip, underarm, and pubic hair should not be referred to as "natural", but "Neanderthal."*

1:00 p.m.: Last Christmas, I had blogged about different holiday shapes that I could leave on the bikini area. One idea was mistletoe. It seems like a perfect spot for a kiss to take place. So the last time this client was in the salon (which was months ago), she said she wanted mistletoe left on her body, but she really did not have enough hair to leave any distinguishable design. When we were tossing around other ideas, she told me that her boyfriend had seen a woman with a mustache design left on her bikini line, which actually made a lot more sense in this case. So I left my first-ever mustache. After staring at if for several minutes to ensure its symmetry and shape, I realized that it looked like Christmas holly. I was so excited that I had come up with a new design. But then I stared at in some more and realized that it actually looked like a Halloween bat. Wrong holiday, but it was the thought that counts.

1:10 p.m.: Menopausal women often bring some interesting conversation and responses in the wax room. Several things can stimulate hot flashes in women. Coffee, hot sauce, and red wine are common contributors. But what about Brazilian bikini waxing? It appears that waxing can also act as a catalyst for the all-consuming, sweltering heat that radiates through an entire body for no apparent reason and whenever the hell it wants to. When this woman started sweating profusely, she asked to remove her sweater. That is when I noticed that her entire bikini area had gotten bright red and started sweating as well. *"We have the ability to make women hot in more ways than one!"*

1:20 p.m.: Honest declarations are good no matter how strange they may be. When I rolled this client onto her side, she told me that I had put her in one of her favorite sexual positions. That felt a little awkward. But, then again, since she was comfortable in that position, I was able to thoroughly wax that area.

1:30 p.m.: This woman had never gotten a Brazilian before. She told me that her husband was very excited to see what it was like. As she was leaving the salon, I told her that her man would not be able to stop touching her. She told me that she did not give a shit about her husband; she was looking forward to touching herself.

1:45 p.m.: There are certain things in life that make you feel very competent and very strong. For example, if you have ever taken a Bikram yoga class, you would understand what I mean. It is a ninety-minute class in a hundred-plus-degree room with ridiculous humidity. When the class ends, you feel like a total bad ass. It is so incredibly empowering to walk out of the room on your own two feet, knowing that you did not die. Because, believe me, there are moments during a Bikram class when you contemplate death as the reward. Many women feel the same way about enduring a Brazilian. When this woman told me she felt like a bad ass for making it through the wax, I totally understood where she was coming from.

2:00 p.m.: The woman walked in the room and told me that her husband wanted to know when she was going to see "the miracle worker." Okay, I am flattered, but I will leave that description to Helen Keller. *"Not gonna lie, but sometimes when we see a messy backside, we wish we had some of Helen Keller's disabilities."*

2:10 p.m.: The last time I heard from this client was through an email. She had been to the dentist, and he gave her some "waxed tutti-frutti" dental floss. The name of the floss reminded her of me, and she sent me a message to tell me just that. I love hearing that strange things like dental floss remind people of me. I think it would be fun to create a whole line of health products that were provocatively suggestive. The possibilities are endless. I think I need a good agent.

2:20 p.m.: Two sisters brought their mom in for a wax. She was whining from the moment she came into the salon about the peer pressure from her girls. They came into the room for moral support, although I think they were making sure she finished the service. She was screaming from the moment the wax touched her stomach. It was not an easy feat to get her to keep her legs open, and it was also difficult to rip the strips off properly since she was continually grabbing a variety of my body parts. It was also nearly impossible to keep her left leg up because she was pushing it so hard against my back. I actually had to ask her daughter to hold her right leg up so I could complete the service because she was not cooperating, and I was getting very frustrated. At one point I removed a strip, and her entire upper body fell off the table and onto her daughter's lap, and her leg pretty much flattened me at the same time. When I asked her to roll on her side, the yelling and the gyrations intensified. Her daughter kept yelling at her to be careful that she did not kick me in the head again. When I told her she was done and that she could get off the table, she said, "That wasn't so bad." Maybe not for her!

When I was editing this part of the book, it just so happened that this client had come back for her second Brazilian just days before. She walked into the salon alone, and I just started laughing because she had not brought her entourage with her. Although she giggled a lot, she did fabulously the second time, and the wax went off without a hitch.

2:30 p.m.: I was talking to this girl about the *Two and a Half Men* episode where Walden gets a Brazilian. There are several things we agreed on. First, we would both like to get Ashton Kutcher naked. Second, we think that scene would have been really fun to film. Third, all men should groom their private parts. Fourth, why wasn't I the one giving him the wax? And, finally, how thankful she was that I do not put my clients on their hands and knees.

2:45 p.m.: When a woman is really scared that the wax is going to hurt, I like to start by waxing "the happy trail" because there is not as much feeling there, and it is a good place to get the client used to the heat and the sensation of the actual ripping. After waxing that area on this client, I commented on how it was not as scary as she thought. She told me that her stomach was all fat, and she knew it would not hurt to wax her fat. It was the other part that she was terrified of.

3:00 p.m.: I have known this woman for over twenty years. I used to do her nails, and I was her personal trainer for a while. Now I periodically wax her eyebrows. She bought eight copies of my first book for her book club. She asked me to come to the club the following month to surprise her friends.

58

So the following month I showed up at her house for the book club. I walked into the house, and the first woman who saw me said that I looked really familiar. The hostess said that I was the author of the book they read that month. The lady said, "If I knew that the author was coming, I would have read the fucking book!" It was so funny. I know that women rarely read the books at book clubs. It is more of an excuse to drink wine and gossip. As it turns out only two women actually read the whole book, and two read a little bit of it. They did have questions for me, and we laughed a lot, and I was glad I went, even if most of the women did not read my book.

The hostess is a pretty fun and outspoken woman, and I got a message from her the next day thanking me for coming to their book club. She said it was a relief to hang out with someone who is even more outspoken than she is. She continued by saying that part of the reason she thinks I am so funny is that I have no filter. Now it is kind of ironic that I already talked about my filter in this book before she ever said anything to me about it. I know that about my personality and am usually not embarrassed by it. In reality, I do not think I would be half as successful in this business if I had a filter. Besides, filters aren't any fun. *"Filters are for coffee makers dear."*

3:15 p.m.: This mom told me that her teenage son got a really bad pilonidal cyst in his butt crack. The doctor actually had to lance it in order to clear out the infection. The doctor also suggested that he start removing the hair in the area so he could reduce the risk of it happening again. I told her that he needed a "crack to sac" wax, which really "cracked" her up. They actually discussed what measures he would take to remove his hair from that area. I think this needs repeating. Waxing is not a luxury but a medical necessity. Oh, wait—that is where Dr. M.E. comes in handy.

3:30 p.m.: Sometimes I just want to say, "Please don't come for a wax if you're feeling especially gassy. It really makes the service quite unpleasant." *"Sorry, darling,"* Raul said, *"but I left the room after the first bout of toxic gas filled the air."* God, I wish I had left with him.

3:45 p.m.: Okay, girlfriend, do you really think that closing your legs is going to make it hurt less?

4:00 p.m.: This woman told me that she knew it was time to see me when her pubic hair never felt dry and she was tempted to use her blow dryer on it.

4:15 p.m.: *"You need to take your underwear off."*

"Can't you work around it?"

"No, I would rather not get wax on your underwear."

"I don't care if you get wax on it."

"But I can't wax parts that I can't see."

"That's okay if you miss some."

"No, it is not. That is where bad reviews online come from. And I get really upset when people post negative reviews."

"I would never post any bad reviews about it."

"At some point I will see your entire vagina, so your underwear will not really do anything but get in my way."

"Are you sure I need to take off my underwear?"

"Are you sure you really want a bald pussy?"

4:30 p.m.: People often ask me if I always wanted to do this for a living. It is a funny question because I never heard about Brazilians when I was in high school or even in college, for that matter. A lot has changed in society, and now "Brazilian" is a household word. So, fortunately, the planets have aligned in my favor, and it is the perfect profession for me. Although I wanted to do a lot of things growing up, extricating hair from women's vaginas was not one of the professions I had ever entertained. I mean who sits in a fifth-grade classroom and tells the entire class that he or she wants to wax pussies for a living? I am guessing not many. *"Telling the nuns in Catholic School you wanted to wax pussies for a living would have been a great way to get kicked out so you could have gone to public school."*

4:45 p.m.: I love waxing pregnant women, especially when the babies move during the service. Often the woman has to readjust her position, like in this case, because the baby moved so much that she became very uncomfortable lying on her back. But, no worries, I was able to finish the service with her lying on each one of her hips. There was no way that I was not going to finish. I have to make sure the doctor can distinguish between the woman's vagina and the top of the baby's head.

5:00 p.m.: My day is winding down, and I am secretly hoping for some easy waxes to come in to finish off my final hour. Unfortunately, that passing thought jinxed me, and I knew as soon as this woman walked in the room that I would have to dig deep for some extra strength and perseverance. She had a really big Afro, and the first thing she said was that it had been almost a year since she had been in to see me. I asked her if she had been shaving or trimming the area. She said she had not touched it. When hair is really curly, there is no definitive direction that it grows in, so I just have to put the wax on in the usual direction and hope it cooperates. Her hair was so dense, however, that the wax was just sitting on top of it and not even remotely sticking to the skin. So I kept petting the strip to increase the heat and friction, and I was secretly praying that I would be able to get the hair out. Every strip that I removed left a ton of stragglers because the hair was so fucking thick. So I had to go back and do each area a second time, which worked beautifully without irritating her skin. Yes, I probably should have trimmed it, but at this point I was too committed to making it work. There was some yelling and some swearing, but after a solid ten minutes of intense concentration and determination, I finished—sweaty, stressed, and exhausted.

61

5:20 p.m.: It seems my praying from the last client is carrying over to this one. She is another one of my countless "Jesus" criers. Women love to call for the guidance of their Lord and Savior during their wax. I have to believe that they call for Jesus when they are climaxing as well.

5:40 p.m.: I am ending my day with an amazingly considerate woman. She felt uncomfortable coming for a wax right after work. You see, she normally comes on Saturdays right after she has taken a shower. So to minimize how sweaty her pussy would get during the day, she cut a hole in the crotch of her pantyhose. Love, dedication... and the pursuit of a happy hoo-ha.

7
Position #2: Porcupine Slayer

One of the reasons so many people are switching to waxing is because hair usually grows back coarse and scratchy when it is shaved. And when hair is that rough and prickly, it can be very irritating to the skin of the person who has shaved as well as the person he or she is intimate with. You have to remember that the skin is actually very sensitive down there, and it doesn't take much for that skin to become irritated. Sometimes when clients do not let their shaved pubic hair grow long enough before coming for an appointment with me, the wax will not even be able to soften the hair enough for me to pull out. Shaved hair can really suck. Over the years I have had men and women use the funniest analogies to refer to that area when it is feeling prickly and irritated, and the following story is an actual conversation that happened via Facebook between a new client and me.

One day I got a message from a girl who said that her man told her that her hair felt like a porcupine when she shaved it. I told her I could tame her wild animal. I asked her to grow out her shaved hair for at least two weeks and then come in to see me. A few weeks later she came in and got her first wax. I have to admit that her hair was indeed quite coarse, but I was able to wax it pretty successfully. The next day I got another message from her. She told me she was thankful that I was such a good porcupine slayer.

Robbins 201

8
Ask M.E. Anything

As you probably can imagine, I get asked a lot of weird shit in my line of work. I really enjoy talking about something aside from all the rain we have had this year or how cold it is in the winter or how little sun we see in Rochester, New York. Go ahead; ask me something juicy or racy or naughty. Even if I do not have an answer for you, I promise that your question will provoke interesting conversation and make both of our days much more enjoyable. And there is really no topic that isn't allowed. The sanctity of the wax room can actually be compared to an adult confessional. *"Why don't you just spit it out and admit that we talk about sex all day long."* Busted.

So here we go. A girl was dating a guy who would not go down on her, so she was hoping that a visit to me would be a part of fixing her dilemma. She said she had brought it up a few times (which had to be awkward), and he just always found an excuse for why he did not want to do it. I cannot imagine what excuses he used and never got around to asking her, which, by the way, is quite unlike me. I am thinking that perhaps he used a head cold or a deviated septum as plausible reasons. So I came to find out that this twenty-eight-year-old man supposedly had never tried oral sex on a woman before. He had received it plenty of times but never even tried doing it (which Raul and I thought was pretty selfish and shitty on his part). So there is a part of me who wonders if he did try it once and the girl told him that he sucked at it, or if he really never did try to do it on anyone. Anyway, she said that this guy was well endowed, so you had to wonder what the problem was. Doesn't he like vaginas? Is he afraid he is going to hurt her? Is he afraid he will not like what it tastes like? Is he really gay? The mystery behind this dilemma will ultimately surprise you. It seems that this good-looking, well-endowed man had a really small tongue. You did not see that coming, did you? He was afraid that he would not be able to pleasure a girl that way. *"My God,"* Raul said, *"she needs to tell that pathetic bastard that the size of his tongue is no excuse."* Fortunately, her approach was much more diplomatic and considerate than my alter ego's. She said that the reason she was getting waxed was so she could go home and teach him how to do it until he got it right. Now that is what I call taking the bull by the horns and getting things accomplished.

Speaking of oral sex, I had a client give me some poignant advice about oral sex one time. She said, "If he doesn't have mojo of the mouth, don't let him go south." Words to live by.

Oral sex seems to be a more prevalent activity since the popularity of the Brazilian wax. And I am glad that I can be such an integral part of women's intimate lives. Thank goodness I figured out to perform this salon service. I have to admit that when I first decided to learn how to do it, I was very close to quitting before I even got started. You need to understand that my ability to perform a Brazilian so efficiently did not become a reality without some agonizing hours of practice. I have had countless clients who want to know how the hell I give myself a Brazilian. Although today I actually find it quite easy, it didn't start out that way. In fact, in the beginning it really sucked. It was a long, arduous, and completely excruciating act that I repeatedly performed on myself in order to get it right. It is actually a miracle that I still have a normal, functioning vagina. A

Brazilian is not something you practice on someone else when you do not have a clue what you are doing. So I had to use myself as a guinea pig when I was trying to learn how to do it. And there was absolutely no way I was going to practice on a paying customer when I had no idea what I was doing. When I learned how to wax, Brazilians were not even in our vocabulary, so there was no one who could have even taught me how to do it. After a lot of trial and error, I was able to perfect the service in a reasonable amount of time. But it did not happen overnight. Now I can actually make myself completely bald in approximately five minutes. But it took a lot of practice, and there was a tremendous amount of swearing and pain involved in the process. So even if I try to make light of your pain and discomfort, I really do understand what you are going through.

The reason that one particular client asked me how I did it was because she tried to wax herself. She said that after an hour there was so much sweat in her belly button that there was no way the wax would even work on any part of her skin. The wax was actually sliding right off her sweaty body. She said that she had put a facial masque on prior to starting the wax, and it proceeded to drip off her face. At one point she wiped the sweat from her face onto the sleeve on her shirt, forgetting that the masque was on her face. She subsequently had the facial product all over her sleeve. She tried to use a hand mirror to see her parts better, but she got so much wax on the mirror that she ended up throwing it out after she was finished. By the way, I think this would make a really funny *Saturday Night Live* skit. I could picture the entire scenario as she was telling me the story, and the only thing I could do was laugh. So after an hour of her self-destruction had elapsed, she decided it was worth every penny to let me wax her.

People have major issues remembering my name, which is part of the reason I go by M.E. Since the name of the salon is Mark &

M.E., my hope is that by using my initials, most people will have an easier time remembering what my name is. It is funny, too, because nobody has a problem remembering Mark's name. Honestly, it really does not matter to me if someone calls me Mary Louise or Elizabeth Mary or whatever name they come up with. It just seems odd that people have so much confusion since my initials are part of the name of the salon. So one day a woman called the salon and asked if I was Elizabeth. I figured I would go with it and said yes. It was close enough. She told me that her girlfriend dared her to get waxed, and she never backed down from a dare. She told me that she was petrified, and I gave her my "it's no big deal" calming speech. She asked me all of the usual questions, including the silly one about whether or not it hurt. We actually talked on the phone for quite a long time. After I answered all of her questions, she made an appointment with me for later in the week. Less than ten minutes later, she called back. It was funny because I recognized her voice immediately and used her name as soon as she started talking, which made her very happy. She said she could not wait two days for her appointment because she was so terrified that she just wanted to get it over with. So we scheduled for later in the day.

When she came in the room, she said she was so nervous all day waiting for the appointment that she felt sick. She asked me again if it was going to hurt, so I reiterated the fact that everyone has a difference tolerance, but I knew she was going to do great. *"It's not a massage, you know. Chances are, when you pull out some hair from its root, there may be a little pain involved."* When I discuss the actual procedure of ripping hair from the genitalia region, it shouldn't surprise anyone that it probably will not be the most relaxing experience of your life. Before I answered her, however, I looked at the massive mound of braids on her head and asked if her hair was real or not. She said it was all extensions. I was so relieved because if that massive mound of hair was real then there might have been a greater chance that her pubic hair was just as massive. Although I briefly mentioned this woman's story in the previous chapter, I wanted to give you the entire scenario from the time she called to the end because it really was amusing. So as I mentioned before, I started right below her navel so she could feel the heat of the wax and get a handle on what it feels like to get waxed on a body part other than her brows. After I finished her happy trail, I commented on how easy it was to get waxed in that area. She said she knew that area would not hurt because she had so much fat on her belly, and she knew she would not have any feeling where all of her fat was. When I got to the front of her bikini line, she said "ow" every time I ripped a strip off. Her "ows" were very loud, so I just kept smiling and tried to keep the conversation fun. In fact she said "ow" every single time I removed a strip from her skin. When I finished, she got off the table and said, "That wasn't so bad. I could do that again." So all of her angst and worry were for naught. It was quick, relatively painless, and even though she complained through the entire service, she really did great. As my momma always said, anticipation is greater than realization. Okay, she probably did not coin the phrase, but she said it a lot.

I often have women who are moving out of town ask me to teach them how to wax because they dread finding a new salon after they leave Rochester. When a client wants me to teach them how to wax themselves, I am more than happy to tell them how I do it. But even if you know the logistics, it is very difficult to attempt to hurt yourself. And when you put the wax on, you cannot be afraid to pull it off. You have to dig deep, find the strength, and rip it like you mean it. In most cases women do not have the balls to rip it off and end up letting the wax dry and picking it off. And picking hardened wax off of any part of the area in question is never a good thing.

I guess the best advice I can give anyone trying to wax himself or herself is to be prepared to make a mess. When I wax myself at home, I put a large beach towel on the floor to protect the wood. I used to have carpet in my bathroom, but I spilled a fair amount of wax on it, and over time it was necessary to put new flooring in. Even professionals make messes, so you really need to be prepared for everything to be sticky. It may surprise you, but wax does not come off anything very easily once it has hardened. *"There should probably be a warning label on every can of wax. If wax is left on any part of the genitalia, an intimate encounter could lead to intense pain and possible disfigurement."*

The next major piece of advice I give women has to do with Band-Aids. Let me ask you a question: can you comfortably remove a Band-Aid from your body without tensing up or without counting to three with your eyes closed and praying you can find the nerve to pull it off? If you answered no to any part of the question then chances are you will not be able to pull a strip off in a successful or efficient manner. So do not even bother.

Buy professional wax. You can buy anything over the Internet so take advantage of our sophisticated technology. Buying cheap wax from a local store will not work as well, will probably hurt a lot more, and most likely will cause your skin a great deal of unnecessary anguish. Some waxes are so poorly made that you risk removing skin in addition to the hair. And that, my friend, will not make your hoo-ha happy. In fact it will make it very, very unhappy. They make waxes for sensitive areas so read the label and spend the extra money. *"You never want to skimp on the snatch."*

Here is one example of what happened when a client tried to wax herself. She came into the room and told me she could not wait to tell me about her home wax experience. She set everything up in her bathroom because she wanted to make sure she had privacy. It is weird to have someone watch you wax that area on yourself. She said it took her a while to get the top part of the bikini line hair-free (about a half hour), but she was able to do it. I was proud of her since most women cannot inflict that kind of pain on themselves. She told me that one of her problems was controlling the wax from flying all over the room. She actually had a real problem cleaning the wax out of the inside of the toilet after she finished. She said she was not really sure how it even got in there because the toilet bowl was across the room. Her biggest problem was separating the lips and holding them apart so she could wax them properly. So her question to me was how she was supposed to hold the curtains apart because they just would not stay separated. Those damn curtains can be so annoying sometimes.

As you can probably tell, I like to educate my clients whenever possible. It must be the teacher part of me that never left my body. But more often than not, my clients educate me. And sometimes I like to share completely seemingly useless and inane information with others just for the pure joy that can be found in it. I totally understand that what I may find important may differ from others, but since you are reading a book about vaginas then I will assume you have similar interests. The following discussion all started because a woman asked me if her pubic hair looked like a merkin, because it was so long. She said she thought it looked like one, but since I did not know what a merkin was, I did my homework, and here is what I found out.

About a hundred years ago, prostitutes used to shave their entire pubic areas to prove they did not have pubic lice (or what we like to call crabs). I think that was a smart idea because who really wants bugs crawling around between their legs? What is really interesting is that a study was recently done that suggests that pubic lice or crabs have become an endangered species because Brazilians are so popular around the world. Now I want you to really think about what I just said. The simple practice of removing pubic hair (aka, the Brazilian wax) has almost completely eliminated a disgusting and annoying sexually transmitted disease worldwide. So I want to put it out there that if you have a desire to nominate me for a Nobel Peace Prize for helping eradicate this awful genital disease, feel free. Once again my name is Mary Elizabeth Nesser, and I will be honored to accept such a marvelous distinction. It is truly humbling to know that I have positively contributed to the eradication of crabs!

Sorry, I did not mean to digress, but I love the idea of getting a Nobel Peace Prize. Not only did prostitutes shave the entire area to keep themselves clean; they would glue hair back on the area to cover up signs of disease, such as syphilis. Isn't that a lovely thought? Let us hide a nasty sexually transmitted disease by wearing a big, fake bush over the infected area. I am not sure if you know this, but Al Capone ended up dying in jail due to complications from a severe case of syphilis. He had a stroke and died of cardiac arrest, but it all stemmed from some nasty shit that was between his legs. Now that does not sound like a fun way to go. Anyway, they called these pubic wigs "merkins." What I really find fascinating is that merkins date back hundreds of years. In today's society, merkins are generally used for decoration, which totally cracks me up because I cannot imagine gluing a wig to the front of my pubic area for any reason. They are also used to cover actors' and actresses' genitalia during nude scenes. I was surprised when I read that they even exist still, but in the right situation I imagine they could be a lot of fun.

When I brought up the topic of merkins in the wax room, I was surprised how many women knew what they were. It appears I was seriously in the minority when it came to my knowledge of this whole pubic wig thing. I could not believe that I had never heard of them before, especially since I have dedicated my professional life to that area. *"Poor, sheltered M.E."* Although I like the idea of using them for decoration, I still can't imagine going into a wig store and seeing a wall of merkins hanging on the wall.

It should not surprise you that I am a huge advocate of keeping your pubic area as clean as possible at all times. In the salon I have a sign in each wax room that tells the clients how to clean up after they get their waxes done. We actually use an oil to remove the sticky residue that is left behind from the actual waxing service. If done properly, you will leave the salon wax- and oil-free because of this three-step cleanup process I have available for each and every client. One day a client said she knew I had a sign, but could I please go over the cleanup instructions with her because she had issues the last time she was in the salon. It appears she did not do a very good job cleaning up during the previous appointment. So I asked her what her problem was. She said she could have tossed a salad in her ass because she used so much oil. *"Oh, that's a pleasant visual,"* Raul responded, deciding to forego his Caesar salad for lunch. It appears she ignored the second and third steps. We read through the instructions carefully, and I am happy to say that she had a much more successful cleanup session the second time around.

I have an incredible amount of dialogue with my clients, which is one of the things that I think sets me apart from other technicians. I communicate on the phone, through texting and emails, and even through Twitter and Facebook. Some of my clients send me the funniest emails when they are looking for appointments with me. A desperate woman in need of a wax usually provides me with some kind of amusing anecdote. For example, I got a message from a woman who said that the song "Welcome to the Jungle" sounds like a manicured lawn at the Roosevelt mansion compared to what was between her legs. Now you have to admit that is pretty funny. But the email continued to get better.

The second part of her message said that I would be able to find Jimmy Hoffa before I would ever be able to find her twat. So I had to get her in that day because her hysterically funny and desperate pleas were enough to have me come in early or stay late or do whatever it took to get the job done. She came in a few hours after I received her emails, and I am happy to say that I manicured her lawn and found her twat. But, no, I did not find Jimmy Hoffa hiding behind her bush.

Sometimes the communication that takes place is more like a counseling session. I have to admit that it makes me feel good to help people with their problems and offer advice whenever possible. The next client was so serious at first that I was worried something really tragic had happened, and in a way it did. She was upset that her rabbit died from overuse. Okay, in case you are confused, I am not referring to a cute and furry little animal that hops around and likes to eat carrots. She was referring to that glorious electronic device that keeps a smile on the faces of women around the world. My advice to her was very simple and straight to the point: give your rabbit a quick burial and buy a new one.

There is also a lot of discussion about what it feels like to have a Brazilian. When a woman tells me that she thinks getting a Brazilian must be what it feels like for a man to get kicked in the balls, I am not sure what to say. I don't have balls, so I don't know what it feels like to be kicked there. I have had countless Brazilians, and I do not think they are that bad. I imagine getting kicked in the balls would hurt way worse. It was a tough question to answer. I hate not knowing it all.

Another person asked me why someone would call the pussy a "pocketbook." I admit that I am not really sure. So I did some research and read some interesting views on the subject. Some people refer to their vaginas as a semidistressed purse, especially after they

74

have given birth. That is obviously not very flattering, and I would hate for any one of my body parts to be described as distressed. It should not surprise you that many women find the reference insulting. I can understand that. Many women do experience changes in their bodies as a result of childbirth, but those changes should be celebrated because they brought life into the world. There are no such things as small miracles, right? Sadly, I have had some women tell me that their men are disappointed in the changes that have happened to their vaginas after they have had a baby. Now this kind of unrealistic and fucked-up criticism of the mother of their children needs to be addressed. If you are with a man with this caveman mentality, please give him the following words of wisdom from yours truly. If he has a preconceived view on what the perfect body should look like and find the changes resulting from childbirth less than perfect, please shove a watermelon in that little hole at the end of his penis and let him see how good that feels. And you can also tell him that his flaccid penis is pretty wrinkly and unattractive, so he really should not throw stones, stretch marks, or any other kind of imperfection in your face.

Let's get back to the pocketbook discussion, because I can feel my blood pressure rising. I know that I keep important things in my pocketbook, such as my license and my credit cards. And my favorite pocketbook just happens to be a Coach bag, which is worth a fair amount of money. More important than the money it cost is the fact that my Coach purse just happens to match my husband's purple car, which makes it even more special to me. In addition, it was the only thing I bought for myself when I went to California for the first time with my two older children. So I guess a woman's pussy is like a pocketbook because it is important to her. She carries it everywhere she goes, and she keeps her things hidden and safe in it, which makes it even more special. So now I can totally understand the correlation between a pocketbook and a pussy. And even though I think men often wonder what women keep in their purses, I think they are even more intrigued with what is in their panties.

One day I had a man ask for my advice. He told me that when his old lady sat naked on the couch, it looked like a raccoon was sitting on her lap. I told him I could kill that raccoon. And I could.

Women ask me all the time why it takes most technicians forty-five minutes to an hour to do a Brazilian. It is hard for me to answer that since it has never taken me that long. I assume that they just do not know what they are doing, do not have much experience waxing, or are afraid to touch that particular body part. I would hate to criticize someone I have not met, even though an hour seems like an exorbitant amount of time. Even when I started doing Brazilians, it never ever took me that long. It makes no sense. It is a small area. Okay, I admit that pubic hair can be really stubborn sometimes, but I repeat: it should never take that long, especially if the sex women are having doesn't even take that long.

Another puzzling question that I get from women is why their men want them to keep some hair down there. In my opinion there are two possible reasons. One, he may not want you to look like a toddler. Men want a woman to look like a woman, and many men find a bald pussy less womanly. That should not bother you. You should find some comfort in it. Secondly, he may be attracted to your pheromones. That is your natural womanly smell that gets him all wound up, provided you are clean, of course. So if he wants a little hair left behind, try it out. As long as the lip and ass hair is removed, do you really care? Those are the parts that feel better when the hair is gone. I think the important thing about this discussion is that he is taking a legitimate interest in your lady parts. I don't think that is a bad thing. Be flattered that he taking that much interest in you and paying enough attention to give his

76

opinion. We will not value his opinion, however, if he decides that he wants you to grow your bush back out and leave it in its natural, ungroomed state. That is not going to work. Some men may not have standards, but we do have standards, *especially when it comes to the state of our snatch.*"

I am constantly getting asked for ways to make waxing easier, and I have so many suggestions in my arsenal that I thought I should write them down. I do have a helpful wax hint page on my website, but I have come up with additional hints that should make your waxing experience more pleasurable. In other words, here is a list that should make your next Brazilian suck a little less.

- First and foremost, thoroughly clean the area in question. It is difficult for any technician to do a good job if she is feeling like she is going to vomit all over your midsection. If you need any advice in this area, please refer to the hygiene chapter in my first book, The Happy Hoo-Ha. The chapter is called "What's That Smell?" In that chapter, I am very specific about how to clean the various parts of your body, inside and out.
- Secondly, do not trim. Although some technicians expect you to trim the area, I get pissed off when you do. Almost everyone trims too short, and then little hairs are left behind that have to get tweezed, and, frankly, I am tired of tweezing. By the way, we call it "tweezing," not "plucking." We tweeze our hair. We pluck chickens. Random but important distinction.
- Drink a lot of water. I am working on your skin, which is comprised mainly of water, so keep

it hydrated and healthy, and your skin will be
thankful.

- Do not drink alcohol before your service or even a
lot the night before. Alcohol is dehydrating, thins
your blood, tightens your pores, increases your risk
of bruising, and makes you much less tolerant. If
you want to get trashed after the service to celebrate, go for it. I have always encouraged having a
good time and celebrating as much as possible.
- Smoking pot also makes you less tolerant. So don't
get high. If anything, getting high increases your
paranoia, which is really obnoxious.
- Do not shave in between. Make the investment one
way or the other. Shaving screws up the whole concept of having your hair grow in finer and thinner.
It also makes my job way more difficult. Waxed
hair is so much easier to remove, which equates to
less pain for you. Shaved hair is usually more difficult to wax, which means more pain for you. *"If
you enjoy the pain, feel free to shave every time between
waxes."*
- Gently exfoliating in between can be helpful as
long as the exfoliating scrub is water-based. Gentle
exfoliation can loosen up stubborn hairs that like
to get embedded in the front of your bikini area
or in the creases of your legs. Do not treat the area
like you are using a cleanser on a dirty pan in the
kitchen, however. Elbow grease is not necessary
and most definitely not recommended. It will only
irritate the fragile skin and potentially cause more
problems with ingrown hairs.

- Use sunscreen on the area when you are in the sun. We need to protect our delicate skin from aging. Wait a few hours before putting any sunscreen on after a wax, however, because it could clog your pores, which will also increase your risk of irritation and ingrown hairs.
- Try to hold still. When you jump, it makes it so much harder on the technician and can cause unnecessary bruising. You can swear like a truck driver or scream like a baby. You can sweat like you are running a marathon or pant like you are giving birth. Just do not close your legs. Try to remember to focus on the area that is getting worked on and be cognizant that I need to physically see it and get at it without trying to move your body parts out of the way in order to wax it properly. Closing your legs makes the whole process longer, more painful, and much messier. And, once again, it is obnoxious.
- Breathe. Holding your breath does not make it hurt less. If anything you will increase your risk of passing out. And, for the record, I do not think that most technicians are certified in CPR. I have smelling salts in my room, but they expired in the 1990s, so I am not sure how helpful they would really be. Try to focus on the benefits you will reap when it is over. Having a baby is very painful. I know because I had three of them. But it is so worth it. It is the same with getting a Brazilian. It only hurts for a minute, but, by golly, it is definitely worth it. So breathe.
- Do not go for a spray tan right after you get a wax. The solutions they spray on you will clog those

pores. Give your skin a day to calm down. But do not go for a spray tan before your wax either, because the stain will wax right off, and you will be left with a large white spot in the middle of your body, which will look ridiculous.

— It is a good idea to wait a few hours after your wax before working out or doing anything strenuous that will cause you to sweat a lot. Perspiration can cause irritation as well as lengthen the recovery time after your wax. Go home, take a shower, and hang out naked. A clean, soft, bald, and naked pussy is just what the doctor ordered.

I have been asked countless times when it is appropriate to bring your child, tween, or teen in for a wax. If your child has pubic hair sticking out of her undies or bathing suit, then it is time. The skin may be a little more sensitive, but nothing is worse than having other kids mock you because you have hair sticking out of your clothes. Shaving will be even more irritating on your child's skin, so you may as well do her a humongous favor and let her get waxed. It may not be necessary to wax the entire thing, but the sides definitely need to be taken care of.

Some things that people ask me are very strange. But I have to admit that it is the strange questions that make my days so interesting. For example, I had a client ask me if I ever waxed a nun. I told her that I do not think a nun would ever get a wax because they do not have sex. Her response was, "Well, that's stupid." *"Think she's on something?"* Raul wanted to know. *"I think it'd be a little sacrilegious for a nun to get her pussy waxed."* I would never say any question was stupid, but that kind of was. In her defense, I think she was just trying to make conversation so she could keep herself distracted from what I was doing, which was actually kind of brilliant.

One of Mark's clients wanted to know if it was smart to promote my political views on my license plate. In case you forgot, my license plate says "WAXITALL." I was confused about his question. I told him that saying something like "wax it all" might lead people to assume that I was liberal, but since I am not seriously involved in politics, the thought of my license plate describing my political views never crossed my mind. The concern over people assuming I was liberal was not what he was talking about. He said that it was obvious that I was "anti-Bush." Okay, that was a good one.

A woman called the salon and wanted to know if "The Home of the Ten-Minute Brazilian" was just a gimmick. I told her that it was actually based on fact. I did tell her that most Brazilians do not take me ten minutes, however. She immediately started to say that she knew it was not an accurate account of the time it took, but I interrupted her and said the average Brazilian actually takes me four to seven minutes. She found that impossible to believe. I told her that it took me ten minutes to do a woman the day before, but the client was thirty-nine weeks pregnant and had gained quite a bit of weight. She said that she got waxed at another salon in town, and it took way longer, so she did not understand how it was possible for me to do it so quickly. I told her that I had twenty years' experience and worked really hard to make it as efficient a service as possible.

She was still not convinced that I was telling the truth and actually insinuated that I did not perform the service properly. She wanted to know if I just slapped the wax on haphazardly and just ripped it off without any consideration of the direction of the hair growth. I assured her that I was performing the service properly, putting the wax on in the appropriate direction, and was not oblivious to the fact that pubic hair grows in different directions. I also informed her that I was indeed an educator and taught people how to wax, so she could feel comfortable knowing that I really did know what I was doing. *"God, people can be so fucking rude sometimes."*

Although she was a skeptic, I think I convinced her that I was not running a scam and that I really did know what I was doing. I tried to explain that since waxing was a painful experience, it was important to perform the service in the most efficient manner. I know many people think that I just rush through the service, but I get Brazilians done as well. I know they hurt. And I just think most people would like them to be over with as quickly as possible.

I would also like to clear something up for the people out there who think I do it just for the money. I have two responses to that accusation. First, when did it become a bad thing to want to make a good living, provide for your family, and be able to afford to send your kids to college? I always thought being successful was something good and positive to work toward. I do not think there is anything negative about success as long as you work hard and are a good person. Besides, if my skeptics made a decent living, I doubt they would apologize for it either. Secondly, if you were face to face with a handful of dirty rectums and gooey vaginas every day, there is no way you would continue to do this job solely for the money. I am faced with some nasty shit on a daily basis, and the only reason I put up with it is because I believe in Brazilians. I think they rock! Enough said.

I had another woman come to me as a referral for a face wax who was also very skeptical of me. She told me what she wanted waxed on her face, so I had her sit in the chair; I turned her face to the side and waxed the one side of her face. She was horrified that I did not take more time deciding where to place the wax. She was also upset that I did not give her warning before I removed the strip. Lastly, she was shocked that I removed the strip so quickly. The woman who normally waxed her face took a long time and turned it into a huge ordeal, I guess. I have a lot of experience and confidence and do not think it is necessary to dwell over an area. She was also used to her wax technician

82

counting before she ripped off the strip. I told her I could not count, but then I realized that sounded bratty, so I assured her that although I had a master's degree in education, I never counted before waxing any body part. I told her that I preferred talking to my clients and not counting to them. She said that she did not like how abruptly I pulled the strip and wondered why I did it that way. I tried to explain that it was important to rip the hair off quickly so the roots all came out.

A couple weeks later, the client who referred this lady to me came in for her usual wax. She said that she heard her friend came in to see me. I told her that I did not think her friend liked me very much. She agreed with me. She said that she was annoyed that I did not spend more time with her and that I ripped off her hair so quickly. I told her that I was aware of her complaints, but I was not going to apologize for how I performed the service because, in my opinion, I did an excellent job waxing her face. So my client asked the "skeptic" what she thought of the wax. She admitted that it was the best wax she ever had.

I am happy to say that she came back for another face wax. She said that although she was skeptical of the way I waxed, she was impressed at how long the hair remained gone. She said that when she went to the other girl, some of the hair normally came back in a few days. I told her that was probably because the last technician she went to did not pull it fast enough, and the hair actually broke instead of getting pulled out by the roots. I told her that my fast and efficient method of waxing tended to work much better, which is why I did it that way. I love when skeptics become believers. I am happy to say she likes me now. And I like her too.

If you remember the title of this chapter, it says that you can ask me anything, and here is another example to show that people really do. I had a couple come together for a wax. The plan was to give the woman a Brazilian and the man a rectal area wax. When I was waxing her, he seemed pretty embarrassed by what we were doing. So he just played with his phone and tried to ignore what I was doing to her on the table. It got more interesting when she asked me if I knew how to have anal sex without it hurting so much. If he was not embarrassed before, you should have seen the look on his face at this particular moment. He looked pretty mortified. Usually women ask me intimate questions like this in private. I was surprised she asked me this in front of him. I told her she could try to find a man with a small penis because then it probably would not hurt so badly. I could not resist saying that with him in the room. But she said she did not like that idea. She preferred it big. He seemed to like that comment. I also told her she should probably buy some anal lube. That seems to help my clients who are into anal sex. She said being wet was not the problem, just the pain. *"TMI already!"* I could hear Raul shout. We discussed changing positions and taking it more slowly. I am not sure if I was able to help or not. Besides, it was awkward having this conversation with her boyfriend in the room. But the funniest part of this exchange is that I thought the guy was going to die from the whole conversation that we were having. He was in his early twenties, and you could tell he was shocked by the frankness of our talk. When I waxed the area in question on her, it looked pretty sore, so that is probably why she asked for my advice. Hopefully she can figure out how to make it work more comfortably for her. I am sure I will find out one way or another. So did I tell you that you could ask M.E. anything?

9

Position #3: Piña Colada Party

I learn a lot from my older clientele. In many instances they are more forthcoming with their experiences and opinions than my younger generation. I was having a sexual lubricant discussion with a woman in her sixties who told me that she liked to use coconut oil as a lubricant. I found this admission very strange. I had never heard of anyone using it for that purpose. Although I have cooked with coconut oil in the past and have even used it on my dry skin, it never occurred to me to put it between my legs. What is really interesting is that since she told me the benefits of using coconut oil, I have had other clients admit to using it as a lubricant as well.

When I learn new things, my mind starts racing. This discussion got me thinking about the possibilities of using coconut oil in bed. All I could think of when we were talking about this was how coconuts reminded me of piña coladas. Suddenly I had visions of a large piña colada with a cute umbrella and a hunk of pineapple and a curly straw growing out of this woman's vagina. So I told her that I really liked the idea of having a piña colada party in the pussy.

10

WTF!

I have to call this chapter "WTF!" because it is the expression that my husband uses when something unacceptable, unbelievable, or inexcusable happens. Many times I cannot share with him things that happen in the wax room because he goes ballistic. When someone has a filthy rectum and the white strip gets covered with brown debris, he just cannot understand how inconsiderate people can be, and it makes him really angry. I have become so accustomed to that happening that it is much easier for me to simply blow it off. The last time I told him about a gross encounter, he said, "What the fuck is wrong with people!" with as much animation as an intense Italian and Lebanese guy can muster. So this chapter is in a way dedicated to him because it is his repeated declaration of frustration that gave me the idea for it. I have to preface this chapter, though, by saying that I really did not want to do a sequel to "What's That Smell?" from *The Happy Hoo-Ha*, but new situations have happened that I just had to share with you. I never thought there would be an original nasty hygiene story, but once again I was wrong. But don't worry; this is not solely a hygiene chapter. I have all sorts of WTF moments that have happened that should entertain you. I'm going to start with a hygiene story, however, because this was a pretty horrific incident that I am still having a tough time wrapping my head around.

Usually I can hide my displeasure when a client comes in dirty. I have had enough unpleasant encounters in the past twenty years that it actually takes quite a bit to startle me. Well, that has officially changed. I am not proud of the following story, but it is interesting enough that I feel compelled to share it. I came across a situation that made me not only yelp, but I was so startled by what was in front of me that I physically jumped away from the woman in fear that whatever I saw in her bush was alive. Yeah, I repeat, I thought it was alive. *"She ain't kidding."*

This woman was very big, and when she was lying on the table, I could not see any of her bikini area because the fat from her stomach as well as her thighs covered it. This is not anything new to me, so I was not worried about what I would find underneath the skin because it is usually just hair and sometimes some tattoos or piercings. I guess I should have been worried, though. The first thing I do when fat covers an area to be waxed is push the skin away so I can see what kind of hair I will be removing. When I pushed this woman's belly back, there was so much mysterious debris in her pubic hair that I yelped, jumped back, and asked her what the hell was in there! *"Not gonna lie,"* Raul said helpfully. *"You sounded like your husband just then."* As soon as I said it, I felt bad about my reaction and tried to mask it with a question. So I asked her if she had used our numbing cream on the area. I prayed that maybe she used too much, and it had dried up and was left as chunks in her hair. I really did not think it was the cream, but I was embarrassed by my reaction and wanted to make the situation a little less awkward. She said there was no cream down there. Then her man, who was standing next to the table, started laughing. Just for the record, this was not funny. At this point, I was still standing at the end of the table, which is where I ended up when I jumped away from her. In fact, I was feeling pretty trepidatious about getting near that area again. I have a pretty good feeling you will be as surprised as I was by what she said was in her hair. She said it was deodorant. Yes, I repeat: she said it was deodorant. I had never heard of anyone putting deodorant in his or her pubic hair, so I repeated the statement to make sure I heard it right. "You put deodorant down there?" She said, "Yep, that's what it is." She continued by saying that a woman needed to stay fresh down there, and that was how she kept herself fresh. Now if this is a common practice, I cannot believe that with all my experience with women over the years, I have never heard of it before. I do a lot of overweight women, but I have absolutely never heard of anyone using deodorant in that area. There had to be at least a half-cup of deodorant remains in her hair. And I do not think it was all freshly applied. Some of it was discolored, which made me think that it had been there a while. In fact, when I tried waxing over the area, the shit was flying all over the place. We actually had to vacuum after she left. During one rip, a piece flew down my cleavage, and I thought I was going to throw up on her stomach. At one point I looked at her man standing next to the bed and was thinking, *Dude, if I were you, I would not put my hand, my face, or my cock anywhere near that area*. Of course I did not say that, but how could anyone think that was okay?

My little voice was laughing his ass off, trying to bring some levity to the situation, which was anything but funny. I guess Raul is my coping mechanism sometimes because somehow I did manage to keep my composure. And what choice did I have but to find humor in this? I have never turned anyone away no matter how unpleasant the situation, and it takes a lot to shock me, but this most definitely did. I did feel bad that she was so overweight that she felt the need to put deodorant down there, but what the fuck? She wasn't *that* big. If you are coming to get that area waxed, clean it thoroughly before you come into the salon. Do not bring me a week's worth of built-up debris that is all tangled in your pubic hair. Maybe if the deodorant

89

was all white, I wouldn't have been so shocked, but it wasn't. It was brown and gray and tan…if I was not clear enough, this was by far the grossest situation I have come across to date.

I told a guy and his wife the story of the deodorant girl. Yes, that is how we refer to her now. After I finished my dialogue, which was very animated when I told it because I still have not gotten over the shock, the man told me I was a prostitute. Now, that was a new one. He said I was a prostitute because I will wax anyone. There is probably something to that. Maybe I should have turned her away. But as horrific as it was, I really felt sad that that had become part of her grooming ritual. Besides, once a woman is on the table, I could never embarrass her by telling her to get back off before I had finished the job. So there is that part of me that felt really bad and another part of me that was really grossed out. Sometimes my job is very frustrating, and I feel quite conflicted. Either way, I will never look at deodorant the same way again.

The next time I went for my yearly gynecological appointment, I asked my doctor if he had ever encountered deodorant in a woman's pubic hair. He said no. And you know what? That really pissed me off. He was actually surprised that anyone would allow such a buildup to form in that area. Surprising or not, I told him it was not fair that a woman would clean up that area for him but not for me.

You are not going to believe this, but the very next day an average-sized woman came into the room and said that she wanted my advice about something. She said she has problems with her legs rubbing together (aka, "chub rub"), and she had heard that putting deodorant on your inner thighs could help. Okay, ladies, you are killing me with this deodorant shit! Since this was just one day after the deodorant girl incident, you can only imagine my response. I started out with, "Let me tell you a story…" When I was done, I told her I had never heard of putting deodorant on your inner thighs. And since mine do not rub together that badly, I don't put anything on them. I know some women use baby powder, but I had never heard of deodorant. I do know that even slender women sometimes have problems with their inner thighs rubbing together, and I am not sure what most people do about it. I also told her that I might never use deodorant again because I was so traumatized by the incident the previous day. By the time she left the salon, she also decided that she was going to skip putting deodorant on her inner thighs.

So I guess you can understand why this is a WTF moment for me. Let me see what else I can pull out of the archives…

Some women share the most fucked-up stories about their lives that I often wonder if I should go back to school and get a psychology degree. I have a client who is married and has two boys with her husband. He is mean, has a bad temper, and cheats on her. Doesn't this sound like the perfect marriage? Oh, wait, it gets better. He gets another woman pregnant and has a daughter. The wife is pissed off because she wants a girl. She shows her anger by keeping the boys from seeing him, which is probably a good thing since he sounds like an asshole. He proceeds to get the girlfriend pregnant again and has another girl. Now the wife is consumed with jealousy. She takes him back just long enough so she can get pregnant again. She finally has a girl of her own. Now she has no qualms about sending him back to the girlfriend. In her mind it all made perfect sense. Since she really wanted a daughter, I guess I am happy that she finally had one. But I found the psychology of this situation really unhealthy. I do think that this scenario would do well on *Jerry Springer*, though. *"Who needs Jerry? We could start our own show."*

I always find it interesting how women discover that their men are cheating, and this is one of the most fascinating to date. A girl thought she had a yeast infection, so she went to the doctor to confirm it and get some medicine. It was right before Christmas, and she did not want a yeast infection to ruin the time off that she had from work because she had a lot of plans with her boyfriend. She had the same boyfriend for a few years and thought they were in a happy, monogamous relationship. She went to the doctor to get checked out and then went back to work. While she was at work, the doctor's office called to say that her test was positive. She was confused because they usually do not refer to yeast infections as positive or negative. She asked them what they meant. They told her that she tested positive for chlamydia.

So she called her boyfriend and told him that she just got the strangest diagnosis from the doctor and wanted to know what he knew about it. He played dumb and said that he could not imagine how she got this sexually transmitted disease. She kept probing him about it because she had not been with anyone else for several years, so it must have come from him. You will not believe what he finally came up with. He told her that she must have gotten it from work. He conjectured that when she changed a baby's diaper, one of the babies must have been a carrier from his or her parent. And then she must have touched her private parts after she changed the diaper without washing her hands. Yes, that is how the disease must have spread to her. She made a habit of playing with herself after she changed a poopy diaper without bothering to wash her hands first. It was a brilliant deduction of how this whole scene played out. Not!

She could not believe how preposterous this notion was and started yelling at him to tell her the truth. He finally admitted that he hooked up with someone else. But he insisted that it only happened once, and it really wasn't that bad because he didn't finish. It appears that during the act he realized how much he loved her, and he knew what he was doing was wrong. So he stopped. My little voice reminded me, *"If a man does not finish, it is usually not a voluntary decision. Face it: this prick is full of shit!*" And this girl wholeheartedly agreed.

After she broke up with him, he began stalking her. He must have had a way to track her from her phone because he would show up at the most random places where she was hanging out. One time he brought a date to where she was having lunch, and my client was tempted to go tell the new girl that his cock was infected. That would have been priceless, and I really wish she would have done it. He deserved to be humiliated. At one point he called the girl's mom to ensure her that he had been tested for HIV, and the test was negative. Okay, you may not have AIDS, but you have chlamydia, which you got from fucking someone else. Yeah, that makes it better. Finally the girl could not take his texts, calls, and stalking anymore and told her dad about it. The dad called the guy, and we can only wish we knew what he said to him because the guy finally gave up and left her alone. I am happy to say that she is totally clear of him and of any signs of the disease and has moved on.

The outrageous stories are never-ending. Sometimes I think I will run out of things to say, but my clients will not let me. Clients will ramble on as ridiculously as I do during a wax. I think it is usually due to nerves on their part. As for me, I try to ramble on as a distraction. I also think that our candid discussions are a result of the bonds I have created with my clients, which I absolutely treasure. Either way the conversations are continuous, and that makes the entire experience so much more fun.

So one day a woman comes in after months and months of going with a more natural look. I don't think she groomed the area at all. Since she had incredibly long hair between her legs, I know that the service had to be very painful for her. When I think that a given rip hurts a lot, I like to show the clients the wax strips with the hair on them to reassure them that it is supposed to hurt when there is so much hair. I also like to reinforce how strong they are to handle the pain.

When I showed her the wax strip with all of this long, thick hair on it, she told me it looked like cat puke. I admit I never heard such a comparison before, but she was kind enough to elaborate for me. She said that she hates when she comes home from a busy day at work and all she wants to do is have a glass of wine, and she sees that her cat has puked in the house. Even though she really wants the wine, she knows it is her fault that the cat puked because she decided to save money by buying Friskies instead of Iams. So then she is forced to clean up the cat puke even though it is really disgusting and makes her feel sick. Well, that is what a wax strip full of her own pubic hair reminded her of. Interesting analogy. But by the time she finished her story, I was done with the wax. So the rambling worked perfectly.

But there are certain times when communication is a problem. I had a girl from Taiwan come to the salon for a leg and Brazilian wax. She was attending a prestigious local college and was working on a very academically challenging degree. For the most part we could sort of communicate, although she had a heavy accent, which was fairly difficult to understand. She also had a hard time understanding many of the questions I asked her, and her responses were often completely separate from the conversation I thought we were having. Okay, so I guess communication was limited at best, but I was trying my hardest to keep the conversation going. When I asked her to roll onto her side, she was very confused about what I was asking of her. So I was forced to physically push her body onto her right side, take her hand and put it on her left butt cheek, and show her that I needed her to lift up her buttocks. That went better than expected, although it was a little strange to touch other parts of her body in order to get her in this weird position. Then came the hard part. I needed her to roll onto her stomach so I could wax the back of her legs. She absolutely did not understand what I needed her to do, and we were both getting frustrated. I went to physically roll her body onto her stomach, but she was already on the edge of the table and would have fallen to the floor if I had not stopped myself and held on to her side. There was a part of me that was tempted to drop down to the floor to show her that I needed her to roll onto her stomach, but I was dressed nicely and really did not want to lie down on the wax room floor. It seemed like a ridiculous notion, but I was getting incredibly frustrated. *"And how the hell is she managing to get a master's degree when she cannot even understand what it means to roll over!"* Raul wanted to know. She finally figured it out, but I felt unsettled for hours after she left because it was just so frustrating.

Speaking of awkward, I joined a new gym this year, which I was pretty psyched about because I am the kind of person who goes to the gym four to five days a week. I usually do not use the locker rooms, though, because I prefer to shower at home. This gym has a few amenities that my last one did not have, however, so I decided to check them out. One day I thought I'd try out their steam room. It has this intense eucalyptus smell, which was difficult to adjust to at first, but once I stopped choking I think I kind of liked it. After about ten minutes, I went to the showers to wash off the herbal smell. This is when the WTF part of the story happened.

I wrapped up in a towel and was walking toward the locker where my clothes were. As I turned the corner I came face to face with a naked woman. I actually stopped midstride because I could not believe what she was doing. With her right hand, she ceremoniously separated her wet mound of pubic hair in three deliberate movements. She then proceeded to use the communal hair dryer with her left hand to blow dry not only the front of her bikini line but underneath as well. I must have looked like a deer in headlights

95

because she looked at me, tossed the hair dryer on the counter, and briskly walked away.

I truly cannot understand why anyone would think that using a public hair dryer on her pubic hair is an acceptable practice. I saw imaginary bugs and germs jumping back and forth from her pubic hair to the warm air coming out of the end of the dryer. It was horrifying. I came home from the gym and told Mark I had been traumatized in the locker room. At first he was genuinely concerned that something bad really happened to me. But when I told him what happened, he was just as grossed out as I was.

When I first signed up at the gym, before my traumatic locker room incident, I was talking to a guy about what I do for a living. My profession, by the way, always seems to initiate interesting conversation. He told me that a lot of men use the hair dryers on their junk to dry their parts before they get dressed. He said that he is always tempted to tell these men that what they really need is a lawn mower, not a hair dryer. Well, I should have listened to his warning more closely because I then witnessed the same practice in the women's locker room.

When I told one of my clients who also belongs to the same gym what happened, she said that she saw a woman blow drying her underarm hair. Trust me, if I ever see a woman drying her underarm hair, I will have nightmares. I have to say that I understand that not all people want to be bald, and I am totally okay with that. Some hair left on the pubis can be attractive and can make a woman feel more feminine. But I have to draw the line when the hair is so dense and long that it needs an electrical appliance to dry it thoroughly. Men have trickier parts, and I guess I can understand why they would want to make sure it is really dry around the sac before they get dressed, but I think there are certain practices that should be performed in the privacy of one's own home.

Okay, it is time to prepare you for another hygiene story. I can't help it. It still baffles me that I am faced with so much yuckiness after all of these years. I had a woman come in for a wax with wet hair. We love wet hair. It means they took a shower. She came into the room, undressed, and hopped up on the table. When I lifted her leg up, I noticed an abundance of thick, white vaginal discharge oozing out of her vagina. I just tried to clean it up with the wax strip so it did not go flying across the room when I waxed her lips. Besides, the wax will not stick to wet. I know that women have discharge, but there is a reason we ask you to freshen up in the restroom before you get your wax done. At this point, it shouldn't surprise you that my little voice had some forceful commentary. *"Please tell her that she should leave her breakfast at home because yogurt is one thing my girl M.E. cannot stand and will not eat! Furthermore, hasn't her momma ever taught her how to clean her plate before she was allowed to leave the house?"* Obviously she did not.

This is probably one of my most memorable WTF moments and one of the main reasons I decided to write this chapter. One day a really obnoxious client came into the salon. She was so rude that I was not sure if I wanted to smack her or tell her to get the fuck out. Believe me, I rarely feel this way. She was unlacing her boots and asked me with a considerable amount of attitude how I knew that the Brazilian was only going to take ten minutes. I told her (in a very sweet manner) that I do Brazilians all day long and have been doing them for twenty years, and I just know for a fact that is how long they take. She said she did not know how I could guarantee it since everyone is different. I told her that unless she was three hundred pounds or nine months pregnant (which she obviously was not), it would only take ten minutes. *"Who the fuck does this girl think she is, sporting an attitude with someone who is about to put hot wax on her v-j-jay?"* I told her that if I was not confident that it only took ten minutes, I would never have put that expression on my awning at the front of our salon. She said she had a wax before, and it took one and a half hours. I told her that whoever waxed her obviously did not know what she was doing.

So she gets on the table, and the service begins at exactly eleven-twenty, and I make sure to mention the time to her. I even point to the clock. As soon as I get ready to start, I notice a really foul order coming from her. It was one of those dead animals doused in ammonia smells that can seriously knock you out. *It was bad enough she brought attitude to the salon, but did she really have to bring a stinky snatch as well? No wonder it took the other tech so long because she could not deal with her funky smell and was trying to figure out how to breathe in between rips without passing out!* As you probably can imagine, everything about this appointment sucked.

So as I am trying to wax her, she will not keep her legs apart. Just for the record, I cannot wax what I cannot see or what I cannot get to. I continue to struggle to keep her legs apart. She kept rolling away from me. It was a battle from start to finish. So I finally ask her, "Do you really want this done? Because you are making it really hard to me to do my job." She said she was having a conjugal visit with her man in jail, and he wanted her to be waxed. I bet he did. But if he thought for one minute that removing the hair would remove the odor, he was going to be severely disappointed. At 11:27, I whip off my glove so close to her face that I almost hit her with it and said, "Seven minutes." I threw the glove in the garbage and left the room. I am delighted to say that this is one client I have never seen again.

Although no story ever seems that outrageous, when you hear something crazy more than once, you know you see a lot of clients. We had a man come in who said he used to be gay but has decided that he does not want to be anymore. That does not really make sense to me, but I go with it. So inquiring minds want to know the pros and cons of sleeping with women. He said he likes their curves and their softness. He also likes how they smell. He said it is a lot easier to get his penis into their vaginas than it is in some guy's ass. Yep, I am like a bartender, you know, and you can tell me anything. And people will tell me things I may or may not want to hear sometimes. When I asked if there were any downsides to being with a woman, he was embarrassed to tell his tale. It appears he went down on a woman with a yeast infection and ended up getting one in his mouth. I have heard about this before, but it still blows my mind that a guy would not notice something out of the ordinary down there. It even took a course of antibiotics to clear the infection. *"I'm not surprised he didn't just stick with dudes. That would have kept me from the straight and narrow path."*

The WTF moments continue. A woman told me that her husband's clippers got all tangled up in her pubic hair. She said she was screaming because she could not shut them off fast enough or get her hair untangled quickly enough. That is when she realized she was way overdue for a wax. You think?

I am very proud of the stuff that I write. Although it is not appropriate for everyone, I know that I have made thousands of people laugh, and that makes me really happy. I also know that there are a ton of people who wouldn't care about what I write about, which is also fine. The daughter of one of my clients bought a bookstore about an hour from our salon. I gave a copy of my first book to the mom so she could give it to her daughter. I was hoping after she checked it out, she would possibly display it at her store. She thought that the book was funny and decided to display it at her place. One day a patron came in and told her that she found the cover of the book offensive. Now if I had called the book *The Cute Cunt* or *The Silly Snatch*, I could possibly understand an objection, but *The Happy Hoo-Ha* is, in my opinion, a fucking adorable name. And there is not a graphic picture of a real vagina on the cover. There is a sweet smiley face underneath the title that is not even remotely anatomically correct. People seriously need to lighten up.

So this mom says to me that she thinks the woman who found my book objectionable probably did not have a very good sex life. I told her that I think she probably never had sex at all or maybe is one of those women who have never had an orgasm. No matter what her reason, I am sorry that she found the book objectionable.

One night after an extra glass of wine, I fell walking up my stairs and sprained my ankle. It blew up, and I went for X-rays to make sure I did not break it. It was actually pretty funny because when I hobbled into urgent care, the woman behind the desk was embarrassed because she knew who I was. I had waxed her before, which really made her blush. As I said, I had too much to drink, and her vagina was the furthest thing from my mind. So I got my X-rays, and it appeared that I had a severe sprain.

The next morning I went to work on crutches. I was able to wax a lot of my clients standing on one leg for a while, but then the good leg started to hurt. I had a very hung-over woman come in around the time I decided that I should try waxing in a seated position because my right leg was throbbing. Keep in mind that I have never tried to wax sitting down in my entire life. Even after knee surgery I waxed for almost a week with most of the weight on my right leg. So this woman was my guinea pig, and I was really hoping it would work. Unfortunately, she was not being very cooperative in her exhausted and hung-over state. But I really did not want to stand up even though I was having a really difficult time maneuvering myself around her flailing limbs. When I lifted her leg that was closest to me and started to rip off a strip, she wrapped her leg around my head and pulled it into her midsection. If you try to imagine the positioning, you can probably figure out that before I knew it, my head was just about face down in her crotch. So that was the exact moment that I stood back up. My face had never been that close to a woman's crotch before, and I hope it never is again. *"You never know. Some women may like your head down there."*

One day one of Mark's clients saw *The Happy Hoo-Ha* lying on the front table. I sat down next to her for a chat, when she picked up the book and congratulated me for having my children's book published. At first I thought I heard her wrong and asked her what she had just said. She repeated that she saw that I had my children's book published. I assured her that it was not a children's book. She insisted that it was. No, that was not awkward. I asked her to read the title and look at the picture. She did not know what a Brazilian was, which is fine because not everyone does. We have had banners on the front of the salon for over a decade, by the way, advertising that we are "The Home of the Ten-Minute Brazilian Wax," but it is perfectly fine that she never noticed them. The strange thing about this scenario is that I have known her for thirty years, and I guess she never realized what I did for a living. She must have assumed that I still did nails. Anyway, I explained what a Brazilian was, and she dropped the book back on the table like it was dirty.

Not all of the fun, danger, or excitement happens in the wax rooms. Several years ago one of our hairdressers had a stalker. He called the salon almost every day to say how much he liked her shoes, or her outfit, or the way she did her hair. He called from payphones from around the area, so there was no way of finding out who he was or where exactly he was calling from. He even called to say she needed her car washed or that she had a headlight out. He would come up with some explanation of why he called her so often, but he would never say who he was or what he wanted from her. She was a beautiful woman with a large male clientele. It could have been any one of her clients. I think it definitely made her a bit leery when she was working on a guy. There was no way to trace the calls, so Mark and his dad would try to answer the phone as much as possible because the caller was afraid to talk to them and would hang up. I just cannot understand what thrill it could give someone to call another person up and say, "Hey, I like the red shoes you have on today." But for some reason, this man got a kick out of it. He finally gave up on her. She was lucky.

The extent of my stalking that I know of was a man who saw me driving in my yellow Mustang. He put an advertisement in the classified section of the paper saying that he was interested in meeting the woman driving the yellow Mustang convertible with the personalized plates. Since my plates are the name of the salon, I do not understand why he just didn't come to the salon. Or maybe he did, and he realized that I was married to Mark, so he went on his merry way.

This is a bizarre story that fits perfectly in this chapter. I had a client who was new to me but said she had been waxed before. Usually a repeat customer knows the procedure and tries to be cooperative. However, since most technicians take so long to perform Brazilians, I can completely understand why women get so nervous coming to me. This woman was very jumpy, and I was having a hard time keeping her limbs from flailing around. At one point I did a rip, and she jumped up and landed on all fours, doggie style. It was one of the strangest things that had ever happened to me. She was literally turned around on all fours! I did not know what she was doing or where she thought she was going. She actually begged me to let her stay like that for a little while until she gathered her wits about her. It actually took several minutes to get her to turn over and lie back down. For the record, I am not comfortable with any woman kneeling naked in a doggie-style position, especially with her ass pointed directly in my face. *"We are firm believers that anything done doggie-style should be performed in private."*

I love this one. It is actually a cool WTF story. One of my clients was going through fertility treatments and had two eggs implanted. But instead of getting pregnant with one or two babies, she got pregnant with three. More specifically, she got pregnant with three girls. The probability of that happening was very low, but she seemed to beat the odds. One of the eggs split, giving her a set of identical twins. So now she was about to be the proud momma of a five-year-old boy and three baby girls.

I had another client who also got implanted with two eggs and became pregnant with just one child. When I told the second woman the story about the first woman, she was feeling very grateful that she was only having one. The thought of triplets terrified her. When she left the salon, she called her husband. He answered the phone, and she said, "Are you ready to thank God?"

The woman who became pregnant with triplets referred to the babies as Baby A, B, and C. The last time I waxed her before she had them was at thirty weeks. She is a tall woman and carried them very well. She was having some strange pains because of the way the babies were positioned, however. She said that Baby A was pressing against her cervix and causing a lot of discomfort. Baby C was jamming some body part between her breastbones, which freaked her out because it caused pains in her chest. So then I asked about Baby B. She was not exactly sure about Baby B's position. She just knew she was floating around in the middle somewhere.

That day I asked her how things were going. Since she had a toddler at home, she said that she was going to need a vehicle that held four car seats. Earlier that day, she and her husband went shopping for a new car that would accommodate four car seats. She said that they basically needed to go shopping for a small bus.

When she first found out she was having triplets, I asked her how her husband was dealing with the news. She said he was adamant that they did not spend any money on anything. No gifts. Nothing extra. He did, however, start smoking again. Do you blame him? I mean WTF? He was having three girls at one time!

I am happy to say that since I started this book, she has had three healthy babies who weighed more than five pounds each. If you think about it, having three babies at one time who all weigh so much sounds way scarier than a Brazilian ever could.

Most people get pregnant the old-fashioned way, but you need to have sex to make that happen. And when a man does not want to have sex with his woman, there are two possible reasons for it. Either he is having an affair or is secretly gay. Well, now I have a story about why a man does not want to have sex with his woman—and it has nothing to do with another man or another woman. I am confident that the reason will surprise you as well.

The couple in question has been together for around ten years. They own a house and have two children. She wears an engagement ring, but they have not settled on a date to make their union official. When I innocently asked her if they have set a date for a wedding, she responded tentatively and told me that she is unsure if they will ever get married. You know I had to ask her why because I do not think I would continue to wear a ring if I did not want to marry the guy. She started out by saying he was selfish and lazy, and she was not really sure she wanted to stay with him. She gave examples of both, and I was already thinking that I would be frustrated with a man like that. But the story gets more interesting. She said that he never wanted to have sex. In fact, for the past five years, she has had to beg to get it every few months. When she asked him about it in the past, he always complained that he was tired. Now just for the record, this woman works a tremendous amount of hours and is doing all the housework and child rearing, so if anyone should be tired, it should be her. Anyway, she told him she was fed up with feeling unloved and undesirable and wanted to know why he had no interest in having sex. She asked if he was having an affair or simply was not attracted to her anymore. He told her that it was time he was honest with her. Hallelujah, an honest answer! But sit down because his honesty is not what you probably expected to hear. He told her he was addicted to masturbating.

Okay, folks, are you fucking kidding me? So it is perfectly fine to masturbate a half-dozen to a dozen times a day, but you cannot take care of your girl every once in a while? She was so surprised by his admission that she went online and indeed found out that there are people who are addicted to masturbating. She was not happy to find out it was a real compulsion, but she had to give him credit for his disclosure.

She told him she could not live like that anymore. He begged for a chance to do better. She said she had been waiting almost five years for something to change. She thought she gave him more than enough time to figure out a solution to their problem, even though she did not know what their problem was. She knew that he masturbated, which made her feel even lonelier because he was more interested in pleasing himself by himself than having anything to do with her.

I can totally understand being addicted to sex. Sex is fun, and it feels good. But I cannot imagine being addicted to sex with myself. I am truly sorry if he has a problem that is causing him to have a torrid love affair with his right hand, but it is not a relationship that I personally would want to be involved in. *"If I were that woman, I would say goodbye with a wave and not by shaking his right hand."*

Okay, it is time to go back to something unpleasant because I just can't help myself. Shaving can lead to a plethora of problems, which is one of the reasons I am a huge proponent of waxing. There is a condition that can arise called a pilonidal cyst, which forms around a hair and becomes inflamed and painful and often needs to be surgically removed. Several clients have had such cysts removed in the past. They lance the area, clean it out, and stitch it back up. Sometimes the cysts are so large that they leave quite a scar. And when they get lanced, they can smell really bad. One of my clients, a surgical nurse, was told by a doctor that he has to perform at least five to six surgeries a week to help get rid of such cysts. He also said that a good ass waxing could prevent this problem. I love when doctors have my back and support my cause.

If that didn't turn your stomach, listen to this. We have all heard of blue balls, but have you ever heard of blue waffles? This was a new term that I learned about this year. One of my clients, a police officer, told me that a diseased vagina is often referred to as a blue waffle. Since it was another unfamiliar term, I went on the Internet to see if I could find anything about this condition. Be careful what you wish for. When I looked it up online, I almost threw up. You should see all the nasty, graphic photos of diseased vaginas. I guarantee it will freak you out as much as it freaked me out. Now I know that if I ever hear a derogatory waffle comment, it refers to a diseased, discolored, or defrosted-looking vagina. Fortunately, no blue-waffle-type vaginas have ever come in for a Brazilian.

And the waffle talk continues. Another client told me that one of her elementary kids called another child a "twat waffle." Once again, I had to go to the Internet because it was yet another unfamiliar expression. When I looked it up, it said that this was another term for an idiot. The woman who told me about this works in our city school district and has heard the term many times before. Sometimes I feel very sheltered. So I guess if anyone ever calls you anything with the word "waffle" in it, you should smack him or her in the head because it is most definitely not a compliment.

My next WTF story is about fuck buddies. Fuck buddies are very common. I guess "friends with benefits" would be a nicer way to refer to such a relationship, but that is not how most women refer to nonboyfriends who they have sex with. I had a girl tell me that she was trying to break it off with her fuck buddy because he acted like a lunatic. Of course I had to ask her to give me some details. She said that one night after they had had sex, he was so pissed off that she did not climax that he got out of bed and punched a hole in her wall. He was completely outraged that she was not satisfied and acted completely out of control. She told me that it had been a stressful week and that she had a lot on her mind, and she did not care one way or the other if she came, but he could not handle it. I guess he must have felt emasculated, which is ridiculous because a woman is much more complicated when it comes to orgasms. Obviously he did not understand how complex a woman can be and just focused on the fact that he had "failed." She was very frustrated that he took it so personally, especially since it was only supposed to be a "friends with benefits" kind of arrangement and not an emotionally driven relationship. It did not mean that much to her. All she cared about was getting him to pay for the hole in the wall so she could move on.

People say the craziest things when they are on the table. Fortunately I am usually quick-witted enough to respond in ways that keep the conversation flowing and fun. One day a woman randomly mentioned that her cat got a Brazilian wax. Okay, she may be one of my more eccentric clients, but this one took me by surprise. At first I was thinking, *What kind of salon would actually agree to wax a cat?* But then I realized there had to be more to the story. She told me her cat had such long hair that she could not clean herself properly, so she took her to the vet. The vet shaved her entire pubic and rectal area, making it easier for the cat to clean herself. Even veterinarians understand the importance of proper grooming. And if your cat needs to have a bald ass, shouldn't you?

One morning I went on a local radio show. It was very early in the morning, and I was only supposed to be on for a little while to give them a check for a charity event that we had at the salon. While I was on the air, one of my clients called in to say how much better and faster I was compared to most wax technicians in the area. It was very sweet of her to call in, and it was an awesome plug for the salon and for me. As she was talking to the DJ, she mentioned the school district that she worked in. Later that morning when she arrived at work, she was immediately summoned to the superintendent's office. He told her that he received a phone call from an outraged parent who could not believe that she said she got Brazilians on the air. My client works in a fairly conservative, rural district about forty-five minutes from Rochester. He told her that the parent wanted her suspended for her admission of lewd behavior. She wanted to know when good hygiene became an inappropriate or lewd behavior that required suspension or any kind of reprimand for that matter. She made sure he was aware that the phone call occurred before school hours, and it did not take place on the school grounds. As a senior staff member of almost thirty years, she also told him that he'd better be careful about reprimanding her. Not only did she threaten a lawsuit, but she made sure he was aware that I wax a ton of the attorneys in our city, and she knew that she would not have a problem finding one who would take the case.

What I did not understand is why this God-fearing, conservative woman who "tattled" on my client was listening to this particular liberal disc jockey anyway. And what is even more ironic is that before my client called in, we were having an in-depth discussion on the air about bacterial vaginosis and smelly vaginas. I cannot believe this woman did not change the station. You have to wonder if she was hoping to learn something about her own smelly lady parts and secretly wished she could get a Brazilian as well.

There are many people who still believe that we have pubic hair for a reason and that we should not remove it all. Maybe the caller who wanted my girl to be suspended for admission of her radical behavior believes there is something holy about pubic hair. Obviously I am not a fan of anyone who believes in that distorted notion. One day I read an article in the *Huffington Post*, and I would like to share my thoughts on it with you. The argument is that although pubic hair is out of fashion visually, it is necessary for keeping the skin from rubbing together. A woman's lips are smashed between two legs, so I do not see how anything between your legs could not rub together, hair or no hair. For most people, their underarm skin rubs together on a regular basis and is not plagued with any kind of nasty disease due to the friction. Should we keep that hair for protection as well?

They also said that pubic hair was supposed to act as a cushion during sex. I guess the person who came up with that statement does not know about all my female clients who admit that they like to be slammed hard, and the last thing they want is a cushion to soften any of the blows. Cushions are designed for couches, not crotches. Anyone who believes in the cushion idea has never experienced how sensual it is to have skin on skin.

The research that I read also said that the hair helps the air flow so that the folded skin does not stick together and develop a rash. I think keeping it hair-free and clean will also keep it from sticking together, therefore reducing the whole rash thing. One of the articles said that you increase your risk of getting a vaginal infection if you remove all the hair. Once again I think bathing can also help with this concern.

In my opinion, since pulling hair out by the root causes the hair to come in finer and thinner, this baby-fine hair must be healthier on the delicate folds. I think it is coarse pubic hair that is causing irritation on the delicate folds, not the softer and finer hair.

They say that waxing can cause scarring. Unless the technician is doing the procedure blindfolded or with duct tape, I think the risk of scarring is minimal, and it surprised me that they even mentioned it. A properly performed Brazilian wax should cause no scarring, and the risk is minimal. So as you can tell, I love reading articles on waxing and have no opinions about them whatsoever. *"M.E. rocks at supporting her opinions. I think she should run for governor."*

When a girl comes into the room and tells me that she found me online, checked out my website, and read all the reviews about me, I feel pretty confident that she knows what to expect when she meets me. Now if you have not checked me out online, my website is very thorough about my experience, and the reviews are, for the most part, outstanding. So after she tells me that she did her homework before coming in to see me, she rudely asks me if I have any experience. It was her tone that was rude, not her word choice. But it was snotty enough for me to put my guard up and watch my word choice. *"Okay, what am I missing here? She said she checked you out but is asking if you have any experience? She obviously cannot read,"* Raul figured. So I gave her one of my big, toothy smiles like my daddy taught me and told her that not only had I been waxing for roughly twenty years, but I wrote a book on the subject, and I promised to take very good care of her. That shut her up.

We have a three-story farmhouse that we have converted into a salon. The majority of the waxing services are performed on the second and third floors of the house. When you are on the first floor, it is very uncommon to hear anything going on upstairs. One day I was hanging out in the waiting room with our receptionist. All of a sudden we heard loud screaming through the vents. I just started to laugh because women do scream occasionally, and I was happy that,

110

for once, I was not the person in the room causing the screaming. My receptionist, on the other hand, could not believe how irrational the client sounded. That was when she looked at the vents and yelled, "It's not that bad!"

I am so glad that I put a helpful wax hint page on our website because it has helped answer many of the questions women have before embarking on this new wax journey. One of the things that I talk about is trimming. As I mentioned earlier, I do not like people to trim because nine times out of ten they trim too short. And when they trim too short, not all of the hair comes out. And if all of the hair does not come out, I either leave them with a lot of strays, or I have to tweeze forever, which I hate to do. Not only do I not have the patience to tweeze more than a few random hairs anymore, but my hands have become so arthritic that it really starts to hurt after a while. So I had this girl come in with hair that was trimmed too short. It was coarse and stubborn and not all coming out, which totally pissed me off. No, I guess it did not piss me off as much as I found it really frustrating. I did not have the time to tweeze all the strays because it would have taken forever. And I hate for a client to pay for a Brazilian and leave with so much hair. She obviously had not read my helpful wax hint page. When I told her that she trimmed too short, she apologized but then told me why she did that. Apparently she went to another salon, and the technician refused to wax her because her pubic hair was not trimmed, but she still charged her for the service. I thought that was absolutely preposterous. How could anyone in good conscience run a salon that way? It just is not right. If I can't wax some clients because their hair is too short, I would never charge them. And it happens. Women come in all the time with hair that has been shaved, and I just ask them to come back in two weeks. But since her hair was too long, what would it have taken for the technician to trim it? People kill me sometimes.

Don't hate me for going back to hygiene, but I swear it is a never-ending issue at the salon, and I had to share this little exchange. Besides, you didn't think I could end the "WTF!" chapter on any other kind of note, did you? A heavyset woman came in during the middle of the day. It was summer in Rochester, which tends to be very hot and humid. Those two climatic conditions are rarely mutually exclusive in upstate New York, and it is nearly impossible not to get hot and sweaty. As she is taking off her pants and undies, she says, "Don't mind me, but I haven't showered yet today." And you wonder why I have a chapter entitled "WTF!"

11

Got 'Em by the Balls

I decided to reintroduce gentlemen's Brazilians or "brozilians" in the salon because we were getting so many legitimate calls about the service. Frankly, I was tired of turning so many clients away. When I advertised on Facebook that we started to do male Brazilians again, I defined it as waxing the entire pubic and rectal area sans the scrotum. I continued my description of the service by saying that if anyone acted inappropriately, we would wax off his wee-wee. This posting was the most widely "liked" post to date.

For years, I would not do a Brazilian on a man. The ripping of the skin around the scrotum was one reason, regardless of the wax I used. Another is that I did not want to deal with perverts. I heard a saying once that I thought was appropriate in this context: the penis has no conscience. I believe that is a pretty accurate statement. If the man has naughty thoughts coming into the salon, God only knows what I would have to deal with. But now I have decided, as I have gotten older and even feistier, that a man would be an idiot to try something with me. I am a strong woman with an even stronger man who works one floor below me. Try something and you will truly regret it. Besides, I do have a lot of control once I get that dreaded Popsicle stick in my hand.

When I first posted the service online, my Facebook friends independently started a campaign to decide what we should call the service. We got "manzilians," "guyzilians," "brozilians," and "boyzilians," to name a few. We decided to go with "brozilians" because it was a term that I had already come across in the media before. It says "gentlemen's Brazilians" on our price list because that sounds more professional—and I do attempt to remain professional, even though it can be really difficult considering what I do for a living. But the conversation continued at a rapid pace on my page. We had clients suggest that we have a description of the service that says "Sopranos Made Here." It is truly accurate that inflicting pain on that area of a man can cause their voices to alter. It is not that I am at all unsympathetic; I just can't help but laugh when a grown man's voice squeals at an unusually high pitch. One client suggested we call it "crack to sac," which I totally love. The problem with that description is that I do not wax every man's scrotum, so that description was not going to work. Besides, it really only refers to the area between the cheeks and not the bikini line. The best part of introducing brozilians to the public was the communication that transpired among the salon's Facebook friends. It was really awesome and really funny. So now I feel inclined to keep everyone updated on the development of that service.

Doing men is different than doing women. Most men are not very tolerant when getting their genitalia waxed. In fact many really fall apart on me. So my goal in this chapter is to entertain you with some amusing stories about the brave men who have taken their pants off in front of me and allowed me to smother their most prized possession with hot wax.

Before I get too involved in the stories, let me give the guys some advice on how to make the service more enjoyable. Okay, maybe the word "tolerable" would be more appropriate. First and foremost, you want to come in clean. This is something I repeat on a regular basis, and it needs to be repeated. The general public is not a good listener when it comes to proper hygiene. That area needs to be dry. When it is sweaty, which seems to happen pretty quickly with some guys, the wax will not work as well. You need to be hairy. You cannot trim it really short or shave it all off and only give me a few days' growth. Bring me your big boy bush so the hair will wax off more easily. Wear comfortable clothes; your junk seems to be more sensitive than the ladies' undercarriages, so you do not want fitted pants to irritate your parts. And try to relax! Holding your breath could only lead to passing out. If you are all tense, you will feel every hair pull from every pore and more. Finally, do not worry about getting an erection. One rip and that bad boy will shrivel up and run for cover. *"She ain't kidding, man!"*

When we wax the low part of a man's stomach that surrounds the shaft of his penis, we normally just push the penis off to the side. I prefer that the men do not help hold it for two reasons. One, they usually get their hands in the wax at some point, which is annoying and can be messy. Two, I do not want any man to start enjoying holding his penis while I am working on him. That would be too awkward, and I just do not want to put myself in that position. So if I do not let them touch it, it just makes things a little safer and a little easier for me. There are occasions when I ask the client to help, however, but it totally depends on the guy.

One of the first men to come in after we posted it on Facebook was a tall, skinny white boy who was so unusually well-endowed that his penis was not staying out of the way. This ruined my whole theory of not having a man help me out by holding it. There was no choice in this instance but to have him hold it so I could get at the hair that surrounded it. During the service, I could not help thinking that I did not know if I was envious of the girlfriend or fearful for her. Raul, on the other hand, was jealous.

The funny thing about that situation was that the very next man who came for a wax was built completely differently. It was no problem keeping his penis out of the way. It was the size of a chicken nugget.

One day I walked into the waiting area and saw a couple waiting for me, so I sat down to chat with them for a minute before we went into the room. They said they had traveled about an hour to get to the salon, which always makes me a little giddy. When I asked them how they heard of me, the man said he had been following me for years. That always gets me pretty charged as well. He said he followed me on Facebook and liked my posts. I explained to him how I had been keeping a blog for nearly four years and copy and pasted that blog to my Facebook page every day. The wife said that he checks what I have to say in the morning and often reads it to her. Since she had gotten a Brazilian in her hometown and it did not go well, he suggested that they drive to Rochester and try me out.

The wife got a Brazilian first, and then it was his turn. He was a big guy with hair on every square inch of his body but his head. He wanted a "crack to sac wax," which basically refers to the area between your butt cheeks. In fact the "crack to sac wax" has become a fairly popular service at the salon. So that is exactly what I did to him, and he was very brave. When he got off the table to clean up, I could not help but laugh just a little. When you are looking at a man from behind, and he has a layer of fur from his neck to his ankles, it looks pretty funny to see a bald racing stripe down the middle of his ass. But that is what he wanted, so that is what I did to him.

I would like to reiterate something I talked about in the first book. When a man is really hairy, it looks silly to wax the whole pubic area if the rest of the body is covered in hair. It makes the area look like a bull's-eye. So if you plan to wax that area, please use a clipper and trim your legs and stomach. Otherwise, you are going to look ridiculous. The same theory really applies to any body part that

116

you wax. It can look really strange to be bald in one area and have a ton of long hair surrounding it. It is not uncommon for us to recommend that a man use a clipper on other parts of the body so there is more symmetry in his look.

The woman who originally told that guy about me came in a few weeks later. She asked me if I remembered the couple, which of course I did. She said that she saw the guy after his wax, and he was very happy with the results. Neither men nor women like having hair around their rectums, and I am glad more guys are getting this service done. Anyway, he told his friend that it was a really cool feeling to have no hair between his ass cheeks because it gave him more ammunition when he farted. *"Can't decide if that comment is TMI or hysterical?"*

It's interesting how popular it is becoming for men to get the cracks in their asses waxed. I think it is a really great idea because men can seriously grow some hair between their cheeks. It can be difficult to wax that area, however, because they tend to be more timid than women when it comes to lifting up their legs and really spreading it wide so I can get in there. It can also be more difficult because the hair tends to be denser, and I often have to wax some of it more than once in order to get it totally hair-free. When we decided what we would charge for this service, we could not decide what to call it. We also could not decide whether or not we would put it on the price list. We finally decided to call it a "between the cheeks" wax. It was more polite.

So as you can probably tell by now, I have become extremely familiar with all of the private areas of both men and women. Last year I was on a local radio show trying to get some publicity for *The Happy Hoo-Ha*. The lead radio announcer read a part of the book that talked about the size of men's penises. He proceeded to ask me, with all my experience, do women really prefer a larger penis? I had to admit to him that size is important to many women. As soon as I said this, however, I regretted it because the majority of his listeners are men. I was

117

thinking that I probably just insulted thousands of men in Rochester. So I chirped into the microphone really fast before the head of the program could say anything and told his male listeners that I know from experience that some women are built very small down there. In fact many could never physically accommodate a well-endowed man without some pain and discomfort. I continued to appease them by promising that if they were not that big, there were a ton of women out there for whom they would be perfect. Although I felt like an idiot for telling the general public that women prefer large penises, I think I covered my ass pretty well. There really are a lot of women with tiny parts that absolutely could not handle a "big ten-inch."

Now it is time to share some creative penis stories. Although I have absolutely no bias about anyone's sexual preferences or deviances, we definitely have more fun with our clients who stray from the norm. It makes for more diverse conversation and more animated opinions. The following story has been ongoing, and I expect it to continue in the months ahead.

A man who is involved in what some may call an "alternative lifestyle" came in for a wax with a note for us. I eliminated the names on the note, but the rest is for real. It said:

To whom it may concern,

He is my slave and I want everything covered by his boxers removed.
He has been a bad boy so make it as painful as possible as you can for him.
Also you may humiliate him any way you see fit. He will do anything you want him to.
Thank you.
His Master
P.S. I want no hair anywhere under his boxers. Have him naked during the waxing for humiliation.

The note was crinkly and stained with coffee.

It was hard to take this note seriously, and you have to wonder if this was all part of a ruse to see how we would respond. No matter how bizarre the situation, however, we try very hard to remain professional. So we kept the note and waxed his junk.

The next day his master sent us a thank you.

A few weeks later his mistress, not his master (I am not sure if they are the same person or not), sent me an email requesting that I do a more thorough wax on his scrotum. I told her that the area has a tendency to tear, which is why I prefer to avoid it. She did not care. She wanted a more thorough wax even if it might injure his skin. She was actually hoping that it would hurt him since he had been misbehaving. So during the next wax, I waxed it all. And, yes, there were a few small tears that hopefully healed up quickly. They may enjoy injury, but I try my best not to hurt people. A few hours after his appointment, I received a thank you from the mistress for my thorough and complete service.

They promised to brag to their friends about how good we were, so hopefully I will have more stories in the future. I did receive another note a few months later that said how great he looked in his hot pink G-string panty after the last wax. They even offered for me to see how he looks in it when I wax him next time. That really is not necessary, but I appreciated the offer and their enthusiasm.

It is assumed that only younger men get their genitalia waxed, but that is not even close to the truth. I had a man in his sixties come in for a "brozilian." He had been waxed at other salons and was never really happy with the job that was done, so he drove five hours to try me out. You have to love the power of the Internet for someone to find me from the other side of our state. He said he wanted his entire area completely bare. He also told me that he would assume any risk if there was damage done to any of the areas where the skin was thinner and more sensitive. He said his scrotum had torn before, but he did not care if that happened because it healed fairly quickly, and it was totally worth it to have no hair on it. When he took off his shorts, I looked at his penis and said, "Hey, you have a hole in your penis!" First off, you must wonder why I would just blurt something like that out. Believe me, I just can't help it sometimes. I had never seen one before, and it was the first thought that came to me. Besides, he did have a hole in his penis, and if I didn't say anything, it would have been like the big, pink elephant in the room. The fact of the matter is that I had never seen a penile piercing before, and I think his penis looked funny with a hole in it. He said he took out his piercing so I did not get freaked out. I told him it would take a lot more than a hole in his penis to freak me out. When I got home that night, I told my husband that I saw my first penis piercing. (Thank God for an understanding husband.) He told me that was nice. This is just normal conversation at the Nesser dinner table. Then I told him what I said to the guy. He just shook his head at first because he understands how I have a tendency to just blurt things out. He did want to know if I asked him if he was able to pee out of the hole. Good one, babe. Next time.

And the story continues...one night we were out with several other couples, and Mark was telling them that I started waxing men and that I saw my first piercing. One of the guys looked at me and said, "So you saw your first Prince Albert, huh?" I proudly said that I did. That is when Mark asked, "What the hell is a Prince Albert?" We were laughing so hard. He had never heard that expression before. Believe me, it is never too late to learn.

I rarely feel awkward performing the service, but I have felt uncomfortable with some of the conversations that have occurred. A man in his twenties came in for a Gentleman's brazilian. He was college educated and had a full-time job. He was a normal-looking guy and a normal-sized guy. I asked him if he was dating anyone. He told me that he had not had a date in seven years because he did not feel he had anything to offer a woman. It saddened me to hear anyone talk that way, so I did not continue with that line of discussion and moved on to other, more random topics. He insinuated that I was the first one seeing his junk in seven years, which was a little awkward, but I just blew off his remark and continued with my ramblings. He tolerated the wax quite admirably and went on with his day.

About two months later, he stopped by the salon to see if I had time to wax him, which, of course, I did. When I saw him in the waiting room, I was excited that he came back. Most men do not come back a second time. I commented that I was excited he came back for another round. He was absolutely flabbergasted that I remembered who he was. I tend to be really good at remembering faces and stories; I just have issues with names sometimes. And I do not wax as many men as women, so I almost always remember the men. After we discussed how his skin responded to the previous wax and other random topics, I asked him if he had been on any dates. He repeated exactly what he said before: that he did not feel like he had anything to offer a woman. That response really pissed me off. My first thought was, *"What kind of parents does this poor guy have?"* It seems pretty obvious from his response that he has very poor self-esteem. So I asked him if he was an asshole or an axe murderer. *"Real diplomatic, M.E."* He said that he was neither. So I told him that he should be proud that he was an educated man with a full-time job. I also told him that he seemed nice, and he was decent-looking, and he needed to put himself out there and take a chance. I am not sure if he has any older women in his life who scold him like I did, but I could not help myself. I hate the thought of anyone feeling that he is not worthy of love. Everyone deserves to be loved.

A man can act as domineering and masculine as Arnold Schwarzenegger, but when he is lying on my table with his pants off, I am the man. So I had to laugh when a man came in acting all gruff and stoic because I knew it was his way of covering up his nervousness about the service. His wife had gotten a Brazilian earlier in the day with ease, so he decided he wanted to be bald for vacation as well. He had no chest or stomach hair, just a thick happy trail and a decent amount of pubic hair. I wanted to start by removing the happy trail, and he got kind of pissed off. He wanted that left there. I thought it looked kind of funny being hairless below and above the trail, but he was not my man, so I let it go. I skipped the happy trail and started on his lower stomach. After two rips, the man said he did not think he could handle it. I know it hurts, but I totally did not expect him to cave so quickly. I told him that his wife did not flinch one bit when I ripped the hair off her pussy, so he needed to stop acting like a baby and let me finish. I normally do not like being a bully, but sometimes it is fun, and it is kind of a payback for people who are not really friendly when they come in. As I kept going, the poor guy was sweating profusely, looking very pale, and growling. He absolutely did not want to finish, but I did not stop. So many times when a client asks to stop, I will not stop, and then they thank me later and often come back because they love the results. I had to keep going.

When he came down to pay, he asked me when it would stop hurting. I told him that it really should not hurt anymore because his skin was just a little red but actually looked fine. I told him the only thing he should probably be feeling was a little heat. So he asked when the hot feeling would go away. I assured him it would subside in a few hours. Then he asked me if the pain from the wax was like childbirth and you forget it over time. *"What the fuck does he know about childbirth pain?"* Let me just say that as a woman who has had children, I would rather have a Brazilian every day of the week then push another seven-pound baby through my cervix. So I told him that he would absolutely forget, and then I assured him that next time would be easier. By the time he left the salon, I realized he was a very nice guy. I figured he was acting strange when he came in because he was nervous. And he had every right to be.

I had another guy come in with a tattoo of a pair of lips on his ass. Of course I demanded an explanation. There are certain things I have to ask about. I always figure that if a person really does not want to share then they will choose to say nothing. Fortunately he was comfortable telling me the story behind the lips. He said that he used to tell his sister to kiss his ass all the time. One time she told him that if he got a pair of lips tattooed on his ass, she would kiss it. So he got the tattoo and waited for the perfect time. At a large family gathering, he reminded her of the bet. Next thing you know, he dropped his pants, and his sister was forced to literally kiss his ass! Now aren't you glad I asked? I was.

Although I should probably ask everyone to check my work when I am done, I have kind of gotten out of the habit. I work so efficiently that I really do not have time to wait for the client to hem and haw over the one or two strays left behind or if the shape is not 100-percent perfect. On this particular day, however, I had a man check my work after I waxed his junk. He sat up and commented on how much his penis had retracted. I told him it was afraid of me. I think he was embarrassed by how small it looked when he sat up. I am not going to lie. It seriously looked like a cigar nub. In fact he said he had never seen it retract so small. I just made light of the situation, because I knew he was embarrassed. Besides, *"After 30 years with the same man, M.E. really couldn't care less if you have a big penis or not."*

If you want a good laugh about what it looks like when I wax a man, check out the YouTube video entitled "2 Dudes Get a Brazilian." It is a video of when I waxed my son and his friend. It gives you an idea of how men respond to the treatment—and it's pretty funny. My favorite part of it is difficult to hear, so I thought I would share it with you. The friend on the table was freaking out because he was so afraid of the pain. I told him not to worry because no one has ever died getting a Brazilian. That is when the cameraman said, "Well, except that one guy."

The night before I waxed them, they were in my kitchen drinking whiskey. The friend was bragging about how uncomfortable it may be when I see his junk because he claimed it was pretty big. I assured him I could handle his junk. When I was waxing him, I asked him where the big junk was that he was bragging about. He said it was hiding. The cameraman said that his shrinks up and hides from me as well. Now that I have started to wax men again, I can attest to the fact that most penises really do try to disappear on me. *"No matter how well you try to play hide and seek with your junk, she will always find it."*

One of my chapters would not be complete without an "oh-so-pleasant" hygiene story. On a ninety-degree day, I had a new male client come in for a wax. It was my last appointment of the day. When he walked in the door, I asked him if he would like to freshen up. He said he was fine. We went upstairs, and I asked him to undress. He was very nice-looking, but he was also a very large man. When he took his pants off, I could not see the area that I was planning to work on. Once he got on the table, it was easier to assess the task at hand. I had to be careful because he had a lot of irritation in the folds of his skin. I also had to be careful because his inner thighs were severely chafed from years of rubbing together. Another issue that I was faced with was that his scrotum was unusually large, and I do not know if it had anything to do with his weight or the incredibly hot day. *"Not for nothing, but that bad boy looks like one of those flesh colored jelly fish you see on the beach in Florida."*

Whenever I ripped a strip from anywhere on his body, his left testicle would move. It was very strange. It would just rotate a little. *"I wonder if you are being punked, and at any minute Ashton Kutcher is going to come busting through the door."* That may have been Raul's secret wish, and believe me, it would have been a welcome relief. In fact I looked at the door several times because his rotating testicle almost seemed like an artificial part. I had never seen anything like it before. To make matters even worse, I had a hard time getting this guy to talk to me, and I really hate when it is quiet in the room. It makes me uncomfortable, and I always worry that the silence will make the client feel uncomfortable as well, which I would never want to happen. At one point I asked him if he was okay, and he just informed me in a soft, growling voice that it really fucking hurt. I was very happy with myself for finishing the entire area, although I could tell he could not wait to get the hell out of the salon. He told me that his girlfriend wanted him to wax this area. But as he was leaving, he said he would never get a wax ever again.

It's funny because we insist that our female clients freshen up before a wax, but we never thought about what to say to our male clientele. From that day on we have also insisted that our male clients freshen up as well. Sweaty balls can get a little stinky.

So I have a random question for you that a friend of mine asked me: if a woman has a hoo-ha, does a man have a hoo-hang? I am leaning toward the affirmative.

If you are a man coming to the salon for a Brazilian wax, let me warn you now that I am going to touch your penis and your scrotum. It is part of my job. One guy could not handle it when I touched him. Whenever I went to move any part of his anatomy, he would jump. I tried to reassure him that I would not hurt him unnecessarily. I mean the waxing part of the service hurts. How could it not? He jumped from the first rip to the last. It made the service very weird.

I would not be able to write this manuscript if it were not for the nerdy people in this world who were brilliant enough to create such remarkable devices like my MacBook Air. I love my computer. It is light and easy, and I am using it at this very moment. That being said, I had a really nerdy guy come in. I am not sure why he wanted a brozilian because the rest of his body was ridiculously hairy. In addition, he said that he had not had a date in several years. Since prostitution is not legal in New York, I was wondering if he just wanted a woman to touch his hoo-hang. Well, I hope I did not disappoint him any because I moved his penis around like it was a hunk of salami on my cutting board. I am only interested in cleaning it up, though—nothing more.

A young guy, maybe thirty, came in for a chest wax and brozilian. When I wax more than the genitalia on a man, I have him keep his pants on while I wax the other body part. And I always do the other body part first. There is no reason for a man to be naked the entire time until I am ready to wax below the belt. This may sound a little strange, but I kind of look at keeping the pants on as a type of foreplay. If a man cannot handle his back or chest being waxed then there is no way on God's green earth that I am going to be able to wax around his penis. So I give men the chance to experience the sensation of waxing before I move on to the intimate parts. This guy had a chest as hairy as, if not even hairier than, Steve Carrell. It was an absolute bitch to get the hair out. I had to do small sections, and it took much longer than normal. I also had to throw my body weight into each and every rip. I give him credit, though, because he took it like a man. Oh, yeah, he *was* a man!

When he removed his shorts, it looked like his penis was hiding in a mound of overgrown sea grass. The sea grass grew straight to the sky like a wall protecting his precious member. I wanted to cry. I did not even know where to start. At this point Mark sent me a message saying my next client was there. Hopefully the guy did not hear the trepidation in my voice, but I told Mark that I seriously needed a few extra minutes.

The guy actually had a very fit body underneath all of his hair and I thought he looked really good with all of his chest hair removed. But it was such a grueling experience for him, I never saw him again. Even though waxing can be very painful, most women will come back and get it done again. I can't say the same thing about the men I see. *"Isn't that why you always tell people there is a reason that women have babies?"*

Once a man has been waxed a few times, the hair is less dense, and it is much easier to come out. This was the case with my next male contestant. He was older and had been waxing for years. He also kept his other body hair short, which made the genitalia look less goofy when it was bald. While making conversation, I asked him the usual questions: "Are you married?" "Yes, over forty years." I think that is pretty impressive in this day and age. Oh, yeah, but he also admitted that he has boyfriends as well. Okay, I have heard that before. "Does your wife know?" "Yes, we have an understanding." I am impressed with her open mind and give her credit for being so understanding. I don't think I would ever be okay with it, but then again it is not my relationship we are talking about. He told me that his daughter asked him one time if he was gay, and he told her that was a personal question and that he was not comfortable answering her. I guess she got her answer.

After a half an hour with this guy (I waxed a lot of his parts), he said that he felt like he was talking to his psychiatrist. I told him that I was probably a lot cuter than his shrink. He agreed. Even if I weren't cuter, would you disagree with the lady who was putting hot wax on your balls? *"Can you tell that M.E. is pretty confident? Oh yea, and she never shuts up?"*

I love this next story. An older couple drove in from about an hour and a half away to get waxed at Mark & M.E. The woman had been given a copy of *The Happy Hoo-Ha* from a friend. When she finished the book, she had her boyfriend read it. They decided to come in and get side-by-side Brazilians. Most people have heard of side-by-side massages—but Brazilians? Love the concept. I need to work on my marketing for that one. Anyway, they had slept together when they were young then they both got married to other people for nearly forty years and then they both got divorced. They are from a small town and did not realize that they lived only twenty minutes from one another all this time. One day they saw each other at the supermarket and rekindled their relationship. Two years have passed since, and they could not have seemed any happier or any more in love. Their chemistry with and affection toward one another were beautiful.

The actual service went pretty well. She went first. Often the skin is more sensitive as it ages, so she was pretty uncomfortable, but he kept rubbing her head and encouraging her. It was adorable. He showed absolutely no feeling one way or the other when I was waxing him. He had experienced some neurological issues in the past, so he said he did not have the normal sensations in his skin anymore; some of his skin had no feeling at all. They were quick to let me know that he has plenty of feeling where it counts, though. *"We probably didn't need to know that part of the story."*

Before waxing men, I had never seen a penis that was not circumcised. Well, that has changed. I see more uncircumcised penises than I ever thought existed. It never occurred to me when I had boys that I would not have them circumcised. I do not know if it has to do with religion or the fear of hurting the baby, but a lot of men still have their foreskin. There are other men who look like they have had partials. I just cannot tell if the foreskin is there, is not there, or if it was just a "sort of" circumcision. It really does not make a difference to me, however, because there is no hair at the tip of the penis. And if I ever do see hair at the end, trust me, you will hear about it.

So I explained at the beginning of this chapter that I decided to wax men again after years of refusing to do so. The following story is part of the reason I decided to get back into it. A man bought my first book on Amazon and thought I was funny, so he convinced his girlfriend to come into the salon for a Brazilian. She tolerated it pretty well. While he was at the salon, he even bought a copy of the book for her. He said he was not going to share his copy. I thought that was awesome. At the time I was toying with the idea of starting to do men's Brazilians again. This guy had been going somewhere else to get his done, but he was not happy at all with how the girl did it. She was taking forever and was not very thorough. So as he was watching his girlfriend get a wax, he commented that he would really like it if I started waxing men again. He was a nice guy and seemed totally harmless, and I was thinking to myself, *What the fuck? Why not?* That was the day I made the decision to start doing Brazilians on men again.

Before we started waxing men's genitalia, we seemed to be getting inquiries all the time. Men would not only call but email us as well. Now that we actually do them again, it seems like the inquiries have started to wane. It is one thing to call a salon and ask about getting your junk waxed, but what if the salon really says yes? Now you are stuck trying it out, or else we may just call you a pussy.

And just like pussies, not all penises are created equal. Some are longer, shorter, thicker, or skinnier. Some are really hairy, and some are completely hairless. They come in all sorts of shapes and colors. Some are straight, and some are crooked. I came across one that was quite unusual, and I was compelled to ask one of my doctor clients about it one day when she came in. I asked her if she knew anything about penises. She started laughing hysterically and said for some reason that kind of question did not seem even remotely strange coming out of my mouth. I explained how I saw a long, thin, and wiry penis that was profoundly crooked. It actually curved downward in a definitive "C" curve. I was perplexed because I have seen a lot of penises in my lifetime, but I had never seen one like this. Fortunately she was able to explain what I had seen.

There is an unfortunate condition called Peyronie's disease that can be caused from inflammation and build-up of scar tissue and plaque on the inside of the penis. When the buildup occurs, the penis can feel lumpy, or it can become curved. The direction of the curvature depends on where the plaque has built up. Currently, 3 to 9 percent of American men are plagued with this disease. They say that it can be caused by trauma, age, smoking, and diabetes. I felt sorry for the man because it was bizarre-looking, and I have no idea whether or not he has normal function down there.

One day, one of my clients's told me her husband had difficulty having sex, because he had Peyronie's disease. She was surprised that I even knew what it was. His was a result of drug abuse when he was younger. It was the first time I ever met anyone who admitted she was with someone who had this disease. It's incredible all the weird shit that can happen to our bodies.

Now that I have learned about this Peyronie's disease and have seen a few suspicious penises in my career, that actual word has taken on a different meaning to me. For example, I really like Peroni beer, but I feel strange drinking a beer with a similar name to that very unfortunate penile disease. The two words may not seem similar to you, but they are close enough for me to think twice before ordering a Peroni beer. Oh yea, and if you ever decide to look up the disease on the Internet, I think I should warn you that the pictures are really disturbing.

Not all of my stories in this chapter are about penises, but they are all dedicated to men. One day, this cop came in for a back wax. He started whining from the get go. First he said that he would rather be in a fistfight every day of the week and twice on Sundays instead of getting the wax. I thought that was a little extreme, but I went with it. He continued by saying that he has been in fights and knew what he was talking about. I think that was the part where he was proving his masculinity to me. When I got near his neck, which tends to be more sensitive, he said that he would rather be tasered than have me wax that part of his body. He continued by saying that he had been tasered before, and that the waxing was much more painful. There is a part of me that feels bad when I am hurting someone, but I just had to laugh at this guy because not only were his remarks constant, but I thought he was really funny. I also realized that he would never in a million years let me wax his junk.

I think men like to share their sexual exploits with me as much as women do. It makes me happy that even if a person is gay, he or she will feel comfortable sharing things with me. This next story is a perfect example. A guy came in who was planning on hooking up with this really hot guy. I have waxed him several times, and he handles the pain very well. His first order of business was to get a wax by me—and I have to say that I love being an important part of someone's predate ritual. It makes me feel special and important, and it reinforces how significant my service can be in a person's life. Then he planned to go home and trim the rest of his body hair. And then he only had one more thing he needed to do before his date. He needed to clean out his piping. This was an expression I had never heard before. To be honest, I am not sure I needed that bit of information. I actually had difficulty getting the visual out of my head. *"C'mon M.E., what did you think they did to prepare for that type of*

131

intimacy?" I guess I never gave it much thought. I've thought about it a lot since then.

Some men may be uncomfortable admitting that they read what I have to say, but I know for a fact that I do have a very large male fan base. One of my clients went camping for a weekend with three other couples. One night they were all sitting around a campfire drinking and telling stories. All of a sudden her husband got up and said he needed to get something from the camper. He comes back to the group with my first book. He proceeds to not only read for an hour to the group but add his own commentary as well. God, I wish I had been included on their camping trip. I think my stories are much more fun when I tell them in person, because I can be animated. I love hearing other people read my stuff even more. Now that I think about it, I have never heard a man read any of my stuff out loud. That would be awesome. But it could be embarrassing because most of my stories about men are about how I've got 'em by the balls.

12

Give Me Your Ass

Although I am an educated woman and, I guess, what some would call an adult, you would think I would be more careful with the language that I use at work. Sadly, that is not the case. Not only do I use profanity, I say words that make some women cringe. I really do not mean to offend anyone; it is just the nature of my work. I guess when you do what I do for a living, there are some behaviors and some vocabulary that just comfortably correspond to the work you are doing. That being said, if you come in for a Brazilian wax, I am going to wax the hair around your rectum. It is just part of the process. If you are weirded out or embarrassed by that part of the service, I promise that it won't be awkward. A hairy asshole is nasty and needs to be taken care of. I know that I could be linguistically correct and ask to see your anus or your rectum, but to me that sounds even more unnatural. Who does not know what an ass is? And in order to get to the promised land, I need you to stick your ass in my face so I can see what I am working on. I actually had a client suggest that I write a chapter called "Give Me Your Ass." She told me that one of the reasons she came back for a second wax with me was because it was so obvious that I was comfortable performing the service. I guess when I told her to "give me your ass," she knew that she would never meet anyone as nonchalant as I am when I am doing a Brazilian. So

133

I will thank her for the suggestion. Here it is, girlfriend, a chapter on asses.

I totally understand why you may feel embarrassed separating your butt cheeks and sticking that oddly shaped and puckered part of your body in my face, but it has to be done. In my opinion no one should have hair around the rectum. Both women and men should find a way to safely remove all of their rectal hair. Hell, my husband will not even let our dog have hair around his ass! When the hair is long, all sorts of nasty things get tangled in it, and I surely do not want to be cleaning that area on an animal or a person, for that matter. You know, if we were more like baboons, we would not have to worry about waxing our asses because they are naturally, permanently bald. But unfortunately we are not like baboons, so we need to take care of that area. Face it: do you really want to worry about picking dingle berries out of your backside every time you have a bowel movement?

One day I had two women come into the salon for Brazilians. As soon as the first woman got up on the table and I started to wax her, the other one started to undress. I could not help but notice that the second woman was very large and was sporting some bright yellow thong underwear. As soon as I started doing my thing, the first woman was yelling things like "sweet Jesus," "Oh, my Lord," and "woo-eee." She was loud and exaggerated, and I could not help but laugh at her theatrics. Some people lean toward God for the strength to get them through the humiliation and pain. I do not think it really helps any, but if it makes you feel better then call on your Savior. When I asked my God-fearing woman to lift her leg up so I could wax her lips, the second one yelled, "What does she expect you to do, aerobics or something?" As soon as she said this, she fell onto the floor and started laughing like a hyena. It was like a *Saturday Night Live* comedy skit that I really wished I had on film. She fell on her knees with her big ass pointing to the sky in her bright yellow thong and was laughing and snorting as loudly as humanly possible. When she fell to the floor, someone on the first floor of the salon actually commented about the loud crash and wanted to know if it had started to thunder outside. No, it was not thunder. It was a partially dressed woman who fell to the floor and was cackling like a hyena. These two ladies took a long time to finish, but they were a lot of fun. And I do not think I will ever forget contestant number two kneeling on the floor with her ass pointing to the sky, crying over the hilarity of the whole situation.

This story is not over. When the second woman got on the table, she was still laughing nervously and talking about the positions the first woman had been in. She was going on about how black women did not like to sweat because it messes up their weaves. She also said that only white women do yoga and aerobics, and she could not believe that I was expecting her to put herself in such crazy positions. As I started to wax her, it was really hard to hold her fat out of the way, especially since she was squirming all over my table like a fish out of water. I was asking her politely to hold still and try to cooperate, but she was flailing around like a crazy woman. There are so many times when I just want to yell at the client and tell them to be still. *"Actually, it would feel better to say, 'Stop fucking moving so I can do my job'."* Believe me, I have wanted to say that exact thing countless times. But I really try to be as professional as possible, and telling someone to stop fucking fighting me probably does not sound that professional.

This whole scenario was really frustrating because she was making it impossible to not only get to her parts but for me to properly rip off the hair. When I asked her to hold her pannus back (the lower stomach fat that hangs over the pubis), the woman started laughing even harder. The more she laughed, the more her body (or should I say her fat) jiggled, and the harder it was for me to wax any of her parts. She could not believe I called her stomach fat anything besides a "fupa," which was what she liked to call it. For those of you who are unfamiliar with the phrase, it refers to a "fat-upper-pussy-area." I know many women call that area a "fupa," but I personally find that expression very offensive. She was literally snorting when she repeated what I said to her and told her cousin that I called it a pannus. She thought that was the funniest thing she had ever heard. While she held her stomach up, she kept moving all around, and at one point she even set her hands in the wax, which made her laugh even harder. As I said, I really wish I could have filmed this entire incident because you would not believe how incredibly funny and loud these women were. When it was time to lift her leg up, her stomach was in the way, so I had to put her leg on my back. My little voice, on the other hand, was telling me I was crazy to be putting this big, heavy leg on my back because I was setting myself up to get hurt. You have to understand that I was determined to get the service over with! That is when she screamed, "You a skinny bitch, and when you rip that strip, my leg's gonna whip your skinny ass across the room!" She asked her cousin, who had just finished cleaning up and was in her underwear, to hold her leg up because she was afraid she was going to hurt me. I am not going to lie; I was a little worried she was going to hurt me also. When she turned to her side to get her ass waxed, she was laughing too hard to keep ahold of her cheek, and it was also too heavy for her to hold with one hand, so the cousin had to hold her ass up as well. It is always amusing when the client needs an extra set of hands to hold up her ass. Although these ladies were an absolute pain in the ass to wax (pun intended), they were a lot of fun.

When you wax women's backsides all day long, you often find out about the women who enjoy anal sex. It really does not matter to me what any of your sexual preferences are, and if you feel like sharing,

I love to listen. You may get some obnoxious commentary once in a while, but that is part of my charm. I have discovered, however, that I do have to be careful when I blog about anal sex because it seems to make people uncomfortable. I guess liking a post on Facebook about such a topic is a little risky, but people seriously go mum when I make any mention of it. That really cracks me up because if you had any idea how many women enjoy it and like to talk about it, you would be blown away. So if someone tells me to be really thorough back there because it is part of her routine, I am on it.

I have a client who never engages in vaginal intercourse with her man. They actually only engage in anal sex. She has several reasons for it, which make perfect sense. One of the problems is that she is a little stretched out from having babies (I think her kids must have had big heads). And that is not uncommon. It seems impossible that the vagina would not stretch a little after an eight-pound baby passed through it, and sadly sometimes it does. In addition, her man is not very well endowed and has had some issues with that area due to some serious health problems. So when they tried vaginal intercourse, for him it was like poking in the wind. You probably are wondering why anyone would share that information with me, but you have to realize I am like a proctologist and a gynecologist and a psychiatrist and the best fucking bartender in the world, so any and all topics are welcome in my sanctuary. I try to do what I can to make that area as good as possible within the parameters of my job. And sharing such information with me gives me better insight into someone's relationship, which I find fascinating. If the man cannot enjoy her vaginally, and she is comfortable with doing it another way, then I applaud her. Successful relationships are all about compromise in and out of the bedroom.

Now I have to say that even when I remove all of the hair back there, it still may not look all that pretty. Even if it is bleached and hairless, I think most people would agree that it is not the prettiest part of a person's body. But what can make it even less pretty are hemorrhoids. Women get hemorrhoids. Men get hemorrhoids. They do not discriminate. You can be old, young, heavy, or skinny. It does not matter. Shit happens. In fact I would be remiss if I did not mention that shit likes to get all clogged up around the mounds of bulbous skin that grow back there. Instead of being embarrassed by it, let us celebrate the uniqueness of our hemorrhoids and do something fun with them. So I was thinking about creating a picture book. Like snowflakes, no two hemorrhoids are exactly alike, and if you use your imagination, you can compare them to something really interesting. Not only will it take the humiliation out of the equation, it could potentially make them less taboo. So let's look at some ideas I have for this very interesting book that I was thinking about writing.

I had one lady tell me to be careful waxing around the head of cauliflower that was between her cheeks. She insisted that I be as thorough as possible since she was getting married that weekend and did not want any hair back there. I had never heard of them being compared to that particular vegetable, but I was impressed by the analogy. Come to think of it, it really did kind of look like cauliflower. Melt a little cheese on top, and you could get really creative. *"Ugh, gross."*

Some look like bouquets of flowers. I cannot say that I have ever come across a floral-smelling rectal area, but I do not ever try to get that close either. When a hemorrhoid starts to grow, it can look like an inflamed red pea that is ready to burst. Those frighten me a bit. I have had visions of them exploding in my face. I do not know if that is even possible, but the thought has crossed my mind more than once. If they are more of the internal type then the area can look more like a volcano that is about to erupt. Talking about hemorrhoids may seem gross to some, but come on, guys, loosen up; it is a natural thing that can happen to anyone. So why not go with it and come up with an imaginative way to make fun of an awkward predicament? I know Barney, the purple dinosaur, would be proud of my endeavors. It can be fun to use your imagination.

Although the picture book is a creative and funny idea, I am not sure how well the concept would go over with the general public. Can you imagine a picture book of hemorrhoids on someone's coffee table? And what would we call this book? *What Is Growing Out of Your Ass?* No, I don't think that would go over well. So I believe I have come up with the perfect name for our new and imaginative coffee table book. I plan on calling it *Rectal Cornucopia*. If hemorrhoids come in all different shapes and sizes then a cornucopia is the closest thing that a cluster of these bad boys would look like. No matter what we call it, I think it is a fascinating idea. *"I wonder what section we would find such a book at Barnes & Noble. Fine dining, perhaps?"*

Last year, we were approached by a Hollywood production company to do a reality show at Mark & M.E. We were excited about the idea. We made video coverage of Mark, me, and our staff, and we even took footage working on clients. It was a little tricky filming in the wax rooms, but we just pointed the camera at the client's head. In the end they decided that since we are such a popular Brazilian wax salon, it would be logistically difficult to film in the wax rooms. Although I have many clients who probably would have been comfortable with other people in the room filming our crazy discussions and all the theatrics, I think the majority of our clientele would not have been comfortable getting filmed during the Brazilian, especially when I waxed their backsides. *"It sure would have made for some funny TV though."*

My Facebook, email, and Twitter correspondence also keeps me very amused. People are flattering and funny and perverted, and I really appreciate it when they share their thoughts with me. One day I got the most awesome message on Facebook. One of my clients wrote, "You can get a half-assed wax anywhere, but you can get a whole ass wax at Mark & M.E." What a lovely sentiment. I try to be as thorough as possible as quickly as possible. Fast is good, because I really do not enjoy lingering back there.

I had a woman come in who had waited way too long to come see me and shared something very personal about how she was dealing with her overgrown rectal hair. She told me that she had to use the baby conditioner called No More Tears on her ass hair because it was getting all tangled. Yes, she did. I cannot make this shit up.

There are only a few clients whose cheeks I do not wax between, and it is usually for health-related reasons. One girl was begging me not to wax that part. I told her that I hated leaving that part of her body hairy because it felt very unbalanced to me, and I disliked not being thorough. She told me that it did not matter because no one ever goes back there. I had to set her straight on that one and remind her that she goes back there every time she takes a shit. And shitting is better when it does not get all tangled in hair! *What a great argument! You should have been an attorney.*

When I was on the radio talking about my book, we started talking about rectal bleaching. It is a service I do not offer and doubt I ever will. In case you are not clear on what it is, it refers to the bleaching of the skin around your anus, not the bleaching of your rectal hair. Anyway, the disc jockey said his area looked like a red wine stain not because it is dirty; it is just that discolored. I was surprised that he admitted it on the air, but I was glad he did because I thought it was a really funny analogy. When you think about it, I'm not sure if most people even know what color their skin is around their rectums. Have you checked yours out lately?

My clients love to share weird and gross shit with me (pardon the pun) because I have such an open-minded kind of occupation and love to talk about everything. I was having an anal sex discussion with one of my girls when she asked me if I knew what a dirty Sanchez was. I had never heard that expression before. She would not tell me what it meant, but I was pretty sure it had to do with something butt related and I had a funny feeling it was going to be gross. Yep, I was right. I went online and looked the expression up. You have to love the Urban Dictionary. You can learn a plethora of interesting things from it. Here is a perfect example. When a man has anal sex with a woman and then rubs the tip of his penis across her upper lip to make a mustache, it is called a dirty Sanchez. Aren't you glad I shared that one with you?

I learn so many random things from my clients. One day I was talking to a client about some of the nasty shit I have experienced and blogged about. She told me that she was surprised that I had never talked about a Portuguese breakfast. I had to admit that I have never heard that expression before, so I had to look this one up as well. Basically a Portuguese breakfast is when you put eggs and various other ingredients in the anal cavity and allow the heat from your body to cook it. They continue the discussion by suggesting that you eat the mixture by sucking it through a straw. I guess the nagging question is, "who comes up with this shit?"

Clients are always telling me how much they love to get their asses waxed. It is not the actual procedure that people find pleasurable. That is not why they love it. It is more due to the fact that it does not hurt as much as the rest of the area. And it is really nice not having hair back there. But I had to laugh when a girl said, "God, it is such a treat to get my butthole waxed!" Everyone enjoys different kinds of treats.

As you learned earlier, I hear a large variety of confessions throughout my day. One woman told me that she loved taking a shit for two weeks after I waxed her, because she felt so much cleaner and things just slid out much easier without any hair in the way. It is the little things in life that can provide such joy.

The rule of thumb is that you should never wax an area more than once. For the most part, I adhere to this rule. There is an exception, however. If I wax the crack in someone's ass and there is still a lot of hair left behind, I do it again in the other direction. Some people can grow some scary dense hair between their cheeks, and I feel that it is my duty as an American citizen to rid the country of any and all rectal hair. *"God Bless America."*

I noticed that a girl shaved the area around the entrance of her vagina and the inside of her butt cheeks. The rest of her pubic hair was really long. She had a friend in the room with her, and they both started laughing when I asked her why she shaved that particular area. She told me that she had a man out of town who wanted her to send a picture of that particular part of her body to him. She did not want him to think she was not keeping up with her grooming, so she just tried to clean up a little bit of her overgrown bush.

The client I just mentioned is the kind of girl who laughs hysterically as a response to pain. She whined quite a bit and said that she could not believe how much it hurt. We were having a very open discussion about sex, and the conversation could not have been any more frank. Since she had shaved around the rectal area and complained about the pain in that area, I told her that anal sex would probably hurt way more than the Brazilian. *"It's fun to bring up taboo topics."* She told me that his cock was too big to fit in her ass, so that was not even an option. At this point I thought her girlfriend was going to fall out of the chair. I continued with the service when she yelled out that she thought the Brazilian hurt way more than his cock ever could.

I have to admit that I did not think I would have enough material to make a chapter about my experiences with the rectal area, but I guess I was wrong. Once again I had a lot to say. So if I ask you to "give me your ass," just give it to me. I've got your back, or shall we say "backside"?

13

Position #4: Rectal Cornucopia

It is incredible and sometimes disconcerting what can happen to our bodies when we have babies, when we age, or when we least expect it and for no apparent reason. There are often physical changes that are completely out of our control. One of those wonderful changes is the introduction of hemorrhoids to our backsides.

A lot of men and women have clusters of hemorrhoids that just invade their rectal areas. I usually only notice them when they are lying on their sides and they lift up their cheeks so I can wax their anal regions. But there are times when a cluster will be so obtrusive that it is visible when they are lying on their backs and their legs are in the air. I am working on a coffee-table book that is dedicated to the men and women who have had so many different shapes and sizes of hemorrhoids protruding out of their anuses that I felt compelled to provide an illustration in their honor.

14

Oh God, What Will M.E. Say Next?

Thank goodness my husband is a strong and confident man, because his wife has quite a mouth. I agree that my profession leads to more colorful conversation, and I try to show as much decorum as possible, but sometimes, that is hard to do. *"Like when you told that young girl that anal sex would hurt way more than the Brazilian? That was showing an abundance of restraint."* I just want people to lighten up and stop taking life so seriously. So I talk about pubic hair and vaginas and penises and sex. So what? Most people are secretly interested in all those topics whether or not they want to admit it. I believe that they are fun topics that should to be talked about and enjoyed.

Since I do look at genitalia all day, I guess I am a little consumed with that body part, and I tend to notice things that others may not notice. For example, one of my favorite hobbies is kayaking with my sister in the Florida Keys. When we go into the ocean, we can be gone for three or four hours at a time. We love the water, the wildlife, the fresh air and sun, and, most importantly, each other. It is by far one of my favorite things in the world to do. One afternoon we saw something weird sticking out of the water. We used to paddle away from unknown creatures, but we have gotten much braver over the years. When we got closer to it, we realized it was a manatee. It was huge- as long as the two-person kayak. We pulled the boat next to it and started petting it. My sister was petting the head, and I was petting the back. Then it rolled over. We were near a dock where a couple was watching us in complete awe as this huge creature was letting us pet it and actually rolled over so we could pet its stomach. When the manatee rolled over, I screamed, "It has a vagina!" That's when my sister yelled for me to look at the engorged nipples. We assumed that she recently became a mommy because the nipples were so pronounced, but we really weren't sure since we had never been so close to a manatee before. The couple on the dock had a better view from up above and noticed a baby nearby. At that point we were laughing and crying and basically freaking out. You see, neither of us had ever touched a manatee before, and to see it there with its baby was magical. Although we had seen a ton of them in the ocean over the years, we never had the nerve to get close enough to pet one. It was one of the most memorable experiences of my life, and, of course, I couldn't help but yell out that she had a vagina.

One of the other things I noticed about manatees is that they naturally have Brazilians. This one had no hair on her underbelly. It was very smooth and hair-free. Since I was up close and personal with her lady parts, I was able to examine her anatomy more intimately than I could ever imagine. I am not sure if everybody would have noticed that particular detail, but I sure did. It was amazing.

Speaking of animals, did you ever realize that there are a lot of animals that naturally have Brazilians? The sphynx cat, for example, is known for its lack of coat. Some people may think this kind of cat looks a little strange since most cats have fur, but you must marvel at its uniqueness. If we have open minds when we look at an animal that has been created differently then we can see the beauty of it instead of thinking it looks like a skinned rat. Besides, bald men can be pretty sexy, too, you know. But since we are so used to looking at cats with hair on them, I admit that it can be startling to look at.

But I think the sphynx would be a perfect choice for a person who is a supporter of Brazilians. All I know is that it is sure neat to pet a bald kitty.

And don't forget about the baboon. I think in some ways I'm kind of jealous of that particular creature. The baboon is a pretty lucky animal from my point of view. It has hair on most of its body, which is a good thing since it lives in the wild and needs to stay warm. For us, it is a good thing to have hair on our heads and our eyebrows. So we are similarly fortunate creatures in this regard because having some hair is the perfect balance. The baboon also needs some protection from the elements, which we really do not need, so I can't make the comparisons between humans and baboons completely symmetrical. But a baboon is lucky because it naturally has a bald ass. I think that is pretty clever. I wonder what God was thinking when He created this creature: *Let me give this big, hairy ape a bald ass just to make things interesting.* It is a pretty amazing distinction if you really think about it. Since things naturally exit those areas, who would not want them free from hair? I know I do.

Let's move on from my obsession with animals that naturally have Brazilians to some other obscure topics. When my daughter traveled oversees, she had the opportunity to ride on the bullet train, a train in Japan that is known for its really high speed. It has a very sleek design and looks like it would go very fast, which it does. Since I am such a fan of Brazilians and have random thoughts throughout the day about related topics, I would like to share my thoughts on this particular subject. I think men come at us like the bullet train after we have been waxed. It just seems to provoke that kind of response. I am not sure if extra pheromones are released when we are waxed, or men just know how sexy we feel when we get it done, but I do know that it can be a precursor to some seriously hot sex. Whatever the reason, I thought the bullet train and a horny penis

149

were pretty much the same thing. The funny thing about this analogy is that my daughter was kind of pissed that I did not mention my children more in my first book, so I would hate to disappoint her now that I have written a second one. Hopefully my bullet train story doesn't embarrass her, but I think she is pretty used to me by now. Besides, this is really what I thought of when she sent me a picture of it last year. So not only did I mention my daughter, but now everyone knows that she traveled to Japan.

So have you heard about vagina steaming? *"Random topic change. No ADHD here!"* Wait until you hear about his one! I have to preface by saying that even though I am very open minded, sometimes I am blown away by all the weird shit that people do. What is even more fucked up is how much money they are willing to spend on this weird kind of shit. Vagina steaming is a service where you sit naked from the waist down over herb-infused steam and let it penetrate into your vagina for up to thirty minutes. The purpose of this practice (I am really not sure what to call it, so "practice" will have to do) is to ease menstrual cramps, balance hormones and PH, and even fight off uterine cancer. I can understand the cramps because warmth does tend to relax the muscles. I am a little skeptical about the hormones and cancer thing, though. I am not sure how anyone could scientifically study the correlation between those factors, but I am sure somebody somewhere is probably doing just that. If sitting on some hot steam can fight off cancer then bring on the steam!

There are many articles online that tell you the different ways you can steam at home. For example, they suggest sitting on a bucket of boiling water. Of course, there was a warning that if you got too close to the water, you could get burned. That would be unpleasant. Another way to do it is to put a bowl of boiling water in your toilet and take a seat. Good luck finding a bowl that will fit perfectly in your commode. The one that baffled me the most was the picture that showed how they did it at one of the salons. It was a picture of a wooden chair with a hole in it. There were towels around the perimeter, and the steam unit was under the chair. I guess that would probably be the best way to do it, but it looked really unhygienic. Plus I honestly cannot imagine sitting in a room with a bunch of other women steaming our vaginas. That seems pretty awkward in my opinion. But you do have to admit that it would be a really funny sight to see a line of women sitting in these chairs, steaming their v-j-jays at a salon. Now that I have thought about it some more, I may have to talk to Mark about adding this service at Mark & M.E. I could be missing something big here. *"In our conservative city? Good luck with that."*

One time I had a girl tell me she went to the doctor so she could get checked out for a urinary tract infection. When they were discussing the causes of such infections, the doctor asked her if her boyfriend blew air into her vagina. She wanted to know why he would ever do that. She thought that blowing air into that part of your body sounded pretty weird. He said it was a fairly common sexual practice that should be avoided because of the germs that can be spread into the vagina. That gets me back to the practice of the steaming. Can you trust that your vaginal steamer is sanitized to its maximum capacity and will not spread germs into the sensitive folds of your most precious parts? I mean if we have to worry about guys blowing into our vaginas then the steam thing could be pretty risky.

So this steam thing also got me thinking about hidradenitis suppurativa. *"ADHD at its finest"* is Raul's diagnosis. I know that it isn't the next logical thought that would permeate most people's minds after contemplating the benefits of having your vagina steamed, but it was the next thought that came to my mind. Hidradenitis is when you get bumps under your skin. These bumps can be as small as the size of a pea and as large as a marble. Some doctors refer to

151

them as acne inversa, so basically it refers to acne under the skin. These bumps usually rear their ugly little bulges in areas that rub together, like the underarms, breasts, buttocks, and groin. They tend to be painful, and when they break open, they discharge very foul-smelling pus. Are you hungry for some fondue yet? They are usually caused by blocked and inflamed hair follicles. So my thought is if we steamed our vaginas more often then maybe the pores would not get blocked so readily, and we would not have to worry about getting hidradenitis suppurativa. Basically, we would be steaming a different kind of carpet.

While I am in the educating mood, let me tell you about a skin disorder I learned about while waxing one of my clients who just happens to be a doctor. There is this condition call lichens sclerosus, a skin problem that usually appears in the genital and anal region. It starts out as small white spots that tend to be shiny and smooth. Over time they gradually become larger, and the skin often gets thin and crinkled. When this happens the skin can easily tear, which can be very uncomfortable and can scar. There is even a small chance that cancer can develop in this spot. It appears most often in postmenopausal women, but no one has really found a cause for it. I just know that I have to be very careful waxing someone with lichens because if the skin tears, it could scar, and I would hate for that to happen. I thought I would share this random bit of information with you in case any of you have any mysterious white spots between your legs that you are worried about. Sadly, I couldn't come up with anything funny about lichens except that it looks like the word lick, and we like to be licked in that area.

I have come to the conclusion that I think people should worry about their wax technicians more. A girl told me that she gets really tired after her waxing appointments and likes to go home and lie down. Let's talk about getting tired. If you could see the massive mound of hair that I had to extract from her genitalia, you would wonder why I do not take a nap between clients. Don't go so long between appointments, and it will not be so traumatic that you need to lie down afterward. Feel some love for the lady who has been ripping out crotch hair for years and is seriously getting tired. *"Now who's whining?"*

While I am lamenting about my age, listen to this one. One night I was flossing and heard something hit my bathroom mirror. I picked it up, looked at it closely, and realized that it was a piece of my tooth. I completely freaked out and yelled for Mark. He told me the same thing happened to him the year before and that it was a pretty easy fix. I really did not care at that moment that it happened to him, because it was really gross and made me feel really old. I told him that having a piece of my tooth fall out made me feel even older than finding gray pubic hair!

So I went to our dentist. Our regular guy who knows us personally was not available, but I got his associate. She knew nothing about me. For the record, I am not a very good dental patient. I have ridiculous anxiety and did not want to be there. But I had no choice. Anyway, she told me that it would take at least an hour to start the complicated process of fixing my tooth. Unfortunately I had only seventy-five minutes booked off from work. So I asked her if I could quickly call the salon to tell my staff that I would be late for my 3:00 p.m. appointment. When I hung up, she asked what I did for a living. I told her that I did Brazilians and would much rather be ripping a vagina then getting my tooth fixed. I am not sure that she understood what I was talking about. She had no response and showed no emotion. It was awkward. *"Who knows, maybe she'd been hitting the Novocaine, because she just stared at me blankly."*

My bottom teeth are really crooked, so it was hard for her to drill half my tooth away. I also have really bad reactions to one ingredient

153

in Novocaine and will not let any dentist use it on me, so the appointment was a nightmare. She used a numbing agent that did not numb as well, so I could feel every time she hit a nerve, which was constant for over an hour. I was having an intense dialogue in my head through the whole appointment to try to get through it: *I had babies; I can do this. Jesus Christ, this kills! I give myself a Brazilian, and it's no big deal. I hate this fucking lady! I can do this. God, this is hell!* It was a long hour and a half. And to make matters worse, it was only the first step in a three-step process to make me a new tooth. Yep, getting older can be a bitch sometimes.

That reminds me of the vagina-related soundtrack I have been putting together. "Hurt So Good" by John Mellencamp can refer to so many things. I just thought about it because of the dental experience I had. It was funny, because one time while I was waxing someone, that song came on. She thought I had played it on purpose as a joke. *"You wish you were that clever."* And there are so many others that do not refer to pain but would be perfect to play during a wax. "Welcome to the Jungle" by Guns N' Roses is extremely appropriate because of all of the jungles I have worked on in my career. Or what about "Slippery When Wet" by Bon Jovi? That is more suitable for after the wax is complete and the woman is rubbing oil all over her pussy. When you think about it, almost any music can somehow be related to vaginas. Or at least in my mind it can be.

Last summer I spent several days in South Carolina by myself working on this project. You see, with my overactive, random, and often forgetful brain, I need absolute silence in order to write. If there are any distractions I cannot concentrate at all. So I would write for a few hours, then find food, then write, and then work out; it was a good schedule. One morning I went down to a Waffle House for breakfast. Waffle Houses are all over the place in South Carolina. So even though I do not eat waffles (after the story about blue waffles, can you blame me?), I thought I would try a Waffle House out. I figured I could get some eggs there. I have to say that I met some of the nicest people in South Carolina. Everybody was so friendly and hospitable, especially since I was by myself everywhere I went. Anyway, while I was eating, I noticed an elderly couple sitting in a booth next to me. The man was soaking his toast in a glass of ice water. It looked really gross. When I looked at his face, however, I noticed that he did not have any teeth, so the soggy toast made sense. But then the perverse side of me thought that oral sex with a toothless man could be really interesting. I looked at his wife and smiled. *"You're like a horny 16- year-old boy. You know that right?"*

I do not think that I would ever want to own a salon in that part of the country because their diets are so bad. I have never seen so many fried chicken joints in my life. And there are white sauces and cheese sauces and bacon, so much bacon, on everything they cook. I don't mind working on heavy people, but I would not want the majority of my clientele to be heavy because it would be too physically demanding. But that is not my only issue with a fried and fatty diet. Poor diets often lead to way more farting!

I have been tweeting for a couple years now, and, as I've mentioned, I call myself Sassysnatch. I tweet about twats. I really do not tweet about anything personal. I just have some kind of genitalia commentary now and again. I don't think that most people really care if I took a shower or went grocery shopping, so I stick with random observations about the snatch. You can probably tell by the way I write that I have continuous random thoughts. Sometimes I wish my brain would just shut the fuck up, but it never does. The whole tweeting thing has been fun, and it is supposed to be good for business, so I try to be clever on a daily basis. But sometimes that can get tedious. Yet there are times when I feel the need to share. Like when the big guy came in for a wax on the hot and humid day, I had to tweet that sweaty balls really do smell. Because they do.

I have also been keeping a blog for over four years called "Hose Down Your Hoo-Ha." To date, I have not missed one day. I write every morning when I get up. If I do not have access to a computer, I have learned to blog from my phone. I guess it sounds a little obsessive compulsive—okay, maybe a lot obsessive compulsive—but I have had so many people say that they read my blog every morning that I just feel compelled to say something every day. If I am not feeling clever, I will often write a poem about pussies or write something short and sweet like "Brazilians breed confidence!" There are a lot of days when I cannot wait to share a funny or gross story about something that happened in the salon. I post my blog on our salon's Facebook page every day, and that is where I have all the dialogue among our Facebook friends. Recently, a man came across our Facebook page and sent me a message that said my posts were very peculiar. I tried to explain that we are a busy Brazilian waxing salon and that I am a writer who posts my blogs on our page on a daily basis. He replied that he thought I was really funny and planned to follow me. I am sure some people who come across our page think we are perverted or really strange. Some may even take offense to what I write. But I can't worry about it. I love to write about my quirky job; I think it is funny.

Feeling like some M.E. words of wisdom? I think the key to a happy marriage is a happy hoo-ha. Well, it is definitely an important part of it.

I think Brazilians need to be the focal point of a television show. How do you feel about *The Bald and the Beautiful*? Let me give you an example of what I was thinking. Just imagine a formal event where the men are in tuxedos and the women are in gowns. Part of the gossip that goes on during the event is about the women who do not take proper care of their undercarriages. Can't you see women gathered in corners whispering about the ladies they saw in the locker room at the country club who were forced to blow dry their pubic hair because it was so unruly? Today's soap operas are dying a slow, painful death. I cannot believe there are only four left on regular television. So maybe what the industry needs is a more creative and modern approach to soap operas. It is definitely something to think about.

I had another thought. I would like to name a show *Total Crotch Confessions*. The concept, if done properly, could put the *Taxi Cab Confession* guys out of business. I know that the Hollywood entertainment company could not figure out how to film at our salon, but there are many companies out there just dying to try the concept out. The *Cab* people are drunk and nasty, but I agree the confessions are funny. Well, my clients confess funny shit too. They just are not all fucked up when they are spilling their guts. The possibilities are endless.

My life would have been so different if I never mustered up the courage to stop teaching. Making women look like prepubescent girls is a far cry from teaching reading and arithmetic to seven-year-olds. I am a very driven woman, so I wonder where I would have focused my energy. Since I love to write so much, I probably would have tried to write a children's book. I have thought of that before. I love children's literature. If I tried to write a children's book now after all my years of obsessing over pussies, I imagine it would be a lot sassier than it would have been twenty-five years ago. Someone interviewed Mark one time and asked him what he thought about me working at the salon. He said he thought that although I was probably a very good teacher, I was made to do this for a living. I thought that was a very sweet and supportive answer. But you have to wonder what makes me the perfect candidate to wax pussies all day long. I guess the fact that I'm not afraid of nudity is probably a big one. I am outgoing and love to talk, which helps eliminate the potential awkwardness. And although I would never bungee jump or sky dive, I think I am a risk taker. I was waxing women's rectums and labia before people ever knew it was possible. I didn't know if it was socially acceptable, but I did it anyway, because there was a demand for it. Women wanted all of their hair gone. And since I had the means to make that happen, I made it happen.

I know that this next section may be coming from left field. *"You are left handed though, so it makes perfect sense to me."* But you never know what I am going to say next, and that is actually the purpose of this chapter. So just go with it. I think this next stream of consciousness explains why I am good at my job and gives you more insight to why I am like I am. I went to a private school from the fifth to the twelfth grades; it was very conservative and very wealthy. Although my parents lived comfortably, and we traveled a lot, and I never wanted for anything, I never thought we were rich by any means. But, for the most part, we had a happy family, so life was good. I was surrounded by a lot of unhappy, judgmental people at the private school, and I never felt like I fit in. In the fifth grade kids were already talking about becoming doctors and anesthesiologists. I didn't even know what an anesthesiologist was. At that point in my life I wanted to be a truck driver and transport licorice across the United States. It sounded fun and adventurous. My dream was most definitely scorned. There was a lot of pressure to go to college and even more pressure to go to an Ivy League college, if you could get in. I was an average student who was more consumed with dealing with my peers than what college I was going to. I knew I would go to college one day, but it was not my main focus when I was twelve years old. My counselor in high school was convinced that I should go to an all-women's college. Since I had the same boyfriend from the tenth to the twelfth grades, she thought I was obsessed with boys. I was a horny teenager who was in love. Of course I was obsessed with him! When my mother and I met with this counselor, she told my mom that I would greatly benefit from an all-women's college. My mother laughed and said that she would never go to an all-girl's school and would not force her daughter to go to one either. Don't misunderstand me; you all know that I love women, but I never understood the appeal of going to a college just for women. The counselor was offended since she herself had attended an all-women's college, but neither of us really cared. It was not something I was even remotely interested in.

When I look back at that high-school romance, I think my commitment to that boy has a lot to say about my view on relationships. I have been committed to the same man for thirty years. Believe me, my marriage has been one of my greatest accomplishments, and regardless of what that particular counselor thought, that high-school relationship was instrumental to me, and I survived a co-ed college in spite of her.

Sadly, I had a really tough time in both middle and high schools, and I am not sure that I would ever want to go back to that time again. I was one of the unfortunate kids who got bullied for as long as I can remember. It started in elementary school. I went to a public school in our town, and kids were mean to me. I lived in a big house with a pool, and my parents drove nice cars, so everyone thought we were really rich, and kids assumed that I was a snob. When I was given the opportunity to go to a private school in the fifth grade, I was excited to meet kids who were not as mean. Boy, was I wrong. It was even worse in middle school. I really did not fit in. I did not have perfect diction, and I did not dress as preppy as the other kids. Plus my parents did not have impressive jobs. For some reason selling insurance was considered a blue-collar profession, and any type of blue-collar job was frowned upon. Needless to say the transition was much harder than I could have ever imagined.

But I think the real crux of it started in the eighth grade, and I still cannot believe how much crap I put up with. No one ever talked about bullying, so I just kind of accepted that people were mean and that for some reason they were mean to me. But it seemed to go on forever, and I absolutely never felt like I fit in. I honestly do not know what started the whole thing or why it continued for as long as it did. I know people thought that I was pretty and that being pretty was a detriment to my popularity. I never really understood why, but it just was. My son told me he did not understand why people would pick on me because I was pretty. He said pretty girls were usually more popular. That is what you think would be the case, but it was not that way for me. I was not comfortable in the upper-class environment in my school, and I think that helped make me an easier person to pick on. I was definitely a good target. Another thing that set me apart was that I liked to dance. I never enjoyed participating in sports, so I never formed the kind of relationships that kids seem to develop on sports teams. Dancing was a pretty solitary gig for me, but I really loved it, and, frankly, field hockey scared the shit out of me.

So you have to wonder why anyone is targeted. There is never a good reason. I vividly remember kids writing profanity and derogatory statements on my locker in the eighth grade. For most of that year I did not even use my locker. They would write crap in my books if I left them around. It was so humiliating. I remember a senior boy liking me when I was thirteen, which did not help at all. I was a friend of his sister, who was in my grade. That was when the rumors really started. Before that, kids were just plain cruel for no apparent reason except that I was different. The upperclassman was kind of cute and rich and popular, but he was also a senior, and

I do not remember ever liking him in that way. I never even kissed him, so what the fuck? I can remember still being afraid of physical contact with boys at that time. I just was not there yet. But reality does not matter to teenagers. They love gossip and hatred. It makes them feel superior. Well, it was a shitty year. Once I got a boyfriend, things got a little better. But by that point I think the damage was done. I think the bullying really affected me more than I realized. My fibromyalgia symptoms started around that time. Some researchers believe that fibromyalgia is triggered by trauma. I believe that. I know that during the most stressful or unhappy times in my life, my symptoms have been much worse. But my parents were always optimists, and I think I have worked really hard to prove that I can be happy and successful in spite of the haters way back when. And now look at me. I think finding love, happiness, and success was just what the doctor ordered.

I was not sure if I was going to share that part of my life with you because I did not want this book to be focused on my personal life. Besides, there is nothing funny about being bullied. Those kind of stories are what memoirs are for, not a funny book about pussies. But I think my personality is as positive and as strong as it is because of the personal hardships that I have endured. Besides, I know for a fact that many of you can relate to the crap I had to put up with in school. And I think the difficult times in my childhood have made me a nicer person. I was never mean to people. That is not how I was brought up. Thank God I had parents who believed in me and provided me with such a great upbringing because I am not sure what would have become of me if I did not have so much joy and love at home. If that sounds too much like a Hallmark card, get over it. I love Hallmark cards.

So I have picked this quirky profession to not only master but to tell the world about. I wax pussies for a living, and I am really proud of it. I would love to go back to my high school and lecture the students on being your own person and finding a profession that you are passionate about and not being afraid of what others may think. If you are a good person living an honest life, then you have nothing to be ashamed of and you should never have to explain yourself to anyone. *"And fuck anyone who has the audacity to judge you."* Go Raul!

I know that it must be so strange for my children to have a mother who does Brazilians for a living and loves to write about it. But I think it is a lesson on not being afraid to work hard and follow a dream, no matter how bizarre that dream may be. No, this is not what I dreamed about doing my whole life. I did not even know what a Brazilian bikini wax was until I was in my mid-twenties. But when the opportunity to try it happened, I was not afraid of it. I was afraid of the wax that got stuck on my lips the first time I tried to wax myself, however.

God, the first time I waxed myself, it really sucked. I was screaming for Mark to help me get the wax off my lips. He kept rubbing the strip, hoping the friction would warm up the wax so it would stick to the paper and come off. We tried picking it off. It was just a mess. I can't believe I ever tried doing it again. When I teach waxing, I tell the technicians to practice on themselves. You learn really quickly how important it is to not only know what you are doing but to do it fast. It is ironic, but the only part of my body I had a hard time waxing once I knew what I was doing was the upper lip on my face (I thought it was important to clarify what lip I am referring to). I just could not take the pain. I ripped half of one side off and stopped. I remember yelling for Mark to help me, but I really didn't mean it, because I didn't want him touching my upper lip either. In my opinion, that is more painful than the Brazilian. Well, that and the neck. The back of the neck sucks too. I tried that once, so I would know what it feels like, and I never did it again. *"That's why so many of us guys get our hair cut before we get our backs waxed."*

I have been doing more private wax lessons, and I love it. I really do love teaching, and I think I'm pretty good at it. I just have a lot more fun teaching waxing than being confined to an elementary school room with twenty-seven first graders and all of those bureaucratic rules. As you can probably figure out by now, I am not a real fan of people telling me what I can or cannot do. I most definitely have a mind of my own. I hope someday I can do a lot more teaching because there are too many technicians doing a lousy job out there, and I think I can help. Many times it is not their fault. I just do not think they are being taught properly. Although waxing a vagina may take some strength and finesse, it really is not as complicated as you may think. Hell, my husband can do a pretty mean Brazilian. Actually, I think he would be really funny teaching a wax class. I imagine he would use one of my favorite teaching phrases, "rip it like you mean it," because so many technicians pull the strip casually and there is nothing casual about removing pubic hair. The difference between how Mark and I would teach a class, however, is that his class would most definitely include a few WTFs.

So I have shared way more personal shit than I ever expected to, but I think some of it is important in defining who I am and why I have been successful. I think we have a choice to learn from our pasts so we can move forward or just blow it off and try to forget the bad stuff and pretend it never happened. I don't think ignoring any of your experiences is probably very healthy, though. I have never thought that ignorance could be that blissful in the end. Learning from our actions and life experiences seems like the better choice. At least it is for me. So I try to be nice to everyone because I know what it felt like when people were not nice to me. I try not to be judgmental because I have been judged, and it sucks. And I try to be happy because life is too fucking short to waste being miserable.

Since I used to be a teacher, I think it is important to educate whenever possible. So here we go. In ancient Egypt, as far back as 1150 BC, the members of the aristocracy were all about removing their pubic hair. Pharaohs, their wives, priests, and priestesses removed all their hair as a symbol of purity. They believed that having hair was animalistic and impure. I think the purity concept is hysterical because I don't know about you, but I have a lot of impure thoughts when I am bald. Regardless, I think the Egyptians were brilliant.

From what I could find out, the first historically documented Brazilian was in 900 BC. Supposedly the queen of Sheba gave Solomon, the king of Israel, a peek at her undercarriage. They say that after she showed him her lady parts, the two of them became lovers for eternity. Now that is my kind of love story.

Epilation was also an important part of Roman culture. All members of the population would remove their hair, from the aristocrats to the slaves. I feel like I have embarked on a practice that our ancestors from thousands of years ago had already mastered. It is just so exciting how a fairly new and popular trend in our culture is not really new at all. In fact, it couldn't really be older.

Prior to the twentieth century, women's bodies were completely adorned by long-sleeved dressed that covered every inch of their skin, from their necks to their toes. It was not as common for women to be bothered with removing all their hair. After World War I, however, women started showing more of their body parts, so hair removal became an important practice again. I guess it just took a world war for women to wake up and groom themselves properly.

That is the extent of our history lesson today. But the lessons continue...I had the funniest thing happen one day at the salon that

I just have to share with you. I was about to wax a woman in her thirties. She has a few children who are on the younger side. She is fit and trim and appears to be very healthy. As I began to wax her, she told me that she did not put her Ben Wa balls in that day because she was afraid that if she flinched, they would fly out of her pussy and break the window that was at the end of the bed. Now, in case you are not familiar with what Ben Wa balls are, please let me educate you. They are marble-sized balls that can be inserted into the vagina or the anus. Women use them in the vagina for at least three reasons: they can aid in stimulation, increase vaginal elasticity, and aid in bladder control. It only makes sense that strengthening the pelvic muscles would make intercourse more intense. Basically they are another creative way to do Kegel exercises for a sustained amount of time. So when you first try the balls out, it is recommended that you only leave them in for a few minutes at a time and work your way up to several hours. If they are left in the body for too long the first time, there could be a lot of pain, and that would defeat the purpose.

So let's get back to the client. I asked her if she wears them on a regular basis. She said that she does, and so do a lot of her friends. I had to ask why she wears them so regularly since she is younger than I am and her body seems normal and healthy in that area. She told me that she does not want to have to deal with being incontinent when she gets older. More importantly, her husband enjoys how much stronger her pussy is.

I had to blog about my conversation with her because I kept getting visuals of her vagina balls shooting out of her body and breaking the window. The next day I really got to thinking about the logistics of wearing the balls in public. I have to share with you my worries about wearing them at the supermarket, for example. If you are walking down an aisle and all of a sudden the balls start to slip out, what would you do? Would you try to nonchalantly shove them back in and hope that none of the cameras spot you? What if security thinks you are trying to steal something under your skirt? If that happens, I can't even imagine being taken to a back room and trying to explain that you were not trying to steal the expensive truffle mushrooms, but, in reality, you were just shoving these little marbles back up inside your body. My second thought is the fear that they will fall out of my body onto the floor and boing, boing, boing down the Band-Aid aisle. Can you imagine a grown woman in high-heel shoes chasing her balls down the aisle? And after she retrieves them, they would probably be fairly wet and dirty. So now what would she do? I guess she would have to casually drop them in her Coach bag and hope no one notices. But then what if the cameras spot her putting something in her purse? It would be pretty embarrassing if you had to dump the contents of your purse on a counter, and the balls just roll away.

I let my blog followers know how intrigued I was with these Benjamin bad boys, and many were kind enough to share with me where they bought theirs. It appears these balls are more popular than I would have ever imagined. But that got me thinking about what some of the negative effects would be of wearing them. So I went on the Internet to see what I could find out. The first thing I came across was a woman who said that her pussy got so muscular that it could choke a cock to death! I thought that was priceless. I am not even sure where I read that, but I thought her sentiment was hysterical. Wouldn't that be an interesting weapon? Now that I have sparked your interest, you will have to let me know where you get your balls and how they improve your life.

I thought this was kind of a fun chapter, because it would give me the opportunity to regurgitate all sorts of miscellaneous topics that interest me. So the next thing I want to talk about is the HPV virus. I know. I went from Ben Wa balls to a virus that can potentially lead to cancer. But it is an increasingly dangerous health issue in our current society, and I wanted to address my experience with the disease. I have a lot of clients tell me they have the virus, and it really freaks some of the girls out. But it is not surprising with all the women I wax every day that I would come across many who have it. Current research says there are over forty types of HPV that can affect the genital area. That is obscene! The last article I read estimated that around twenty million Americans have HPV. Sadly, having the virus can lead to cervical, vaginal, and vulvar cancers. I am thrilled that they came up with a vaccination, but you have to wonder why more teenagers are not getting it if roughly 74 percent of people infected range in age between fifteen and twenty-four years old. I had my one son and my daughter vaccinated. They did not offer it for my oldest until after he was eighteen years old, and then they wanted to charge a lot for it and said it was not that effective if he was already sexually active. When it first became available for the boys, the doctors really did not push it or give a convincing argument as to why a young man would need it if he could not get cervical cancer, for example. But guys can spread it to girls, which is a pretty convincing argument for why they should get it as well.

When I was doing some research on HPV, I found that it could lead to throat and neck cancers. Then I remember losing a young mom in our community who had HPV in her tongue, and it was the most horrific thing you have ever seen. It had spread throughout her face and was very deforming, and she died much too young. Since then I met a woman who is with a man going through a horrible bout of throat cancer due to HPV. I cannot believe how quickly this virus is spreading. It is really scary.

The rate at which this virus has spread reminds me of AIDS. When I came to Rochester at nineteen years old, I had never heard of AIDS. Everyone I knew was on the pill. No one used condoms because they were annoying. We worried about pregnancy and maybe herpes. We were in college doing our thing and not worried that sex could be a fatal extracurricular activity. It was during that year that I remember learning about the threat of AIDS. I feel the same about HPV now. All of a sudden it has become this vastly widespread disease that is out of control.

When I heard about the guy suffering from throat cancer, I got a little freaked out. So I sent my oldest son an email with information about his scholarship and an upcoming vacation we were planning to take. My final paragraph was a source of education and a plea. I told him about the risk of getting the HPV virus in your mouth and how it could potentially lead to cancer. I also told him about the guy I knew of who was not very old and was going through treatment and could not eat. I concluded my note by saying that the moral of the story was that a young man should be very careful whom he goes down on.

If this seems inappropriate to say to your child, I thoroughly disagree. I know for a fact that he was not aware of the risk that this rampantly growing virus could be to him. He is now a man in his twenties, and I will continue to share with him any knowledge that I think can help him and potentially save his life, even if it is sexual in nature. In my opinion, that is one of the things that moms are for.

It is time to move on to a more humorous topic. This may sound a little strange, but I have to thank a television show for the boost of interest in Brazilian waxing worldwide and the subsequent start of my career as a Brazilian wax technician. The episode of *Sex and the City* that portrayed Carrie getting a Brazilian is what launched my career. If you have not seen it, it can be found on the Internet and is worth watching. If you saw the episode, I think it is worth watching again. It was such a funny scene, and the dialogue was fantastic.

168

So I've decided to share some of the things that are said during that episode.

Carrie thought she was going in for a simple bikini wax. She was horrified when the woman took everything off. She did not even know what to call the service that she had just experienced. She told her friends that she got mugged and that the woman did something unspeakable: she took off everything! She continued by saying that she felt like a hairless dog. I think that is a good thing since hairless dogs tend to be very soft. Samantha advised Carrie that in Los Angeles, everyone took it all off. That is when Miranda said that LA men were too lazy to go searching for anything. Carrie complained that she was bald and freezing. Unbeknownst to her, bald was the objective. And I doubt she was freezing since the area tends to be hot after a wax. The ladies also discussed how you have to be careful whom you invite to Brazil. I agree with that. The climax of the discussion, pun intended, is that she felt like she was so aware of "down there," and she whined that she felt like she was nothing but walking sex. I love when they do skits about Brazilians on television. It should not be a taboo subject. If so many people are getting them, let's share in the pain and the joy and the thrill.

In one of the *Sex and the City* movies, the girls all go on vacation. Miranda had been neglecting that part of her grooming repertoire. When they show her lounging in a bathing suit with an enormous bush sticking out of the sides, I laughed so hard that I cried. And her friends' reactions were just as funny. Even if you have not seen the movie, you should look up that scene online as well.

Although she had a really big, hairy bush in the movie, I have seen much worse. You may think you are the hairiest, but, trust me, you are not. Every day someone complains that he or she will be the hairiest person I have ever seen. Trust me, I have seen hairier. I have told countless women in my career that they are not the hairiest person on the planet and that I have indeed seen hairier. So do not get all worked up about the amount you come in with. It is just hair, and it will be gone before you know it.

This next story is so fun. I have a woman who comes in every couple of months for a wax. She never makes an appointment because it stresses her out, and she knows she will cancel. So when she drives by and sees my car, she will stop in. Every time she will tell me that it is fine with her if I do not have time to do her. So you know I have never said no to her.

One day she actually made an appointment for her and her friend to get it done. I did the friend first. While I was doing the friend, she was yelling at my regular in the hallway about the pain and how weird it was to be getting it done. But my client reassured her that it was totally worth it. She told her that all she would want to do after she left the salon was touch herself. The friend said that she was glad she had no plans for the day so she could spend the entire day masturbating. Their conversation through the closed door was absolutely priceless. I did not even have to participate in their discussion because they were nonstop.

Then my client asked her friend if her husband knew she was getting a Brazilian done that day. She said that he only thought they had gone to breakfast. The woman in the hallway told her that she should sit on his face that night because it would be a great way to let him know what she had done that morning. The friend said he would be totally shocked if she sat on his face and that he would probably have a heart attack if she ever did that. I think you can imagine what my comment was to that remark. I told her that at least he would die a happy man.

Most women do not have a lot of discomfort after a Brazilian. There may be a little redness or the sensation of heat, but for the most part women leave the salon feeling refreshed. I am sure that they also feel thrilled that the service is over. Occasionally women tell me that they feel the need to sit on ice after a wax. I have never experienced the need for ice before, so it is not a practice that even crosses my mind. One day a woman told me that she prepared an ice pack ahead of time so it would be ready when she got home. She told me that she had to sit on ice every time because her vagina swelled up and was really uncomfortable after a Brazilian. When I finished the wax and was leaving the room, I told her to "have a fun ice date!"

I get really annoyed when women think twice about getting a wax because they are self-conscious about their stretch marks. In most cases women have stretch marks because they have babies. And a baby, in my opinion, is worth any kind of mark that is left behind. So do not ever feel embarrassed about your body. Embrace what you have. If you did not have the stretch marks, you may not have your children. And if you have stretch marks because you were once over-weight, be proud of the fact that you have lost the weight. Women tend to be so hard on themselves, and it really pisses me off. *"She's venting again!"* I can hear Raul saying. But he's heard it all before.

A girl once told me that she felt skinnier after she got a wax. I can understand that sensation. There may not be a ton more room in your panties, but it definitely feels like there is. I do have to say that some women come in with such an abundance of pubic hair that I bet they are a little bit lighter when they leave the salon.

So what will M.E. say next? Chances are it is a lot because I have a lot to say. And chances are also that there will be some profanity included in the word choice. So it probably will not surprise you that "fuck" is the absolute number-one swear word said in the waxing room. I hear it from men and women, old and young. One time I had this girl scream, "Fuck balls!" and I thought I was going to wet myself. I was laughing so hard because it seemed like such a strange expression to come out of her mouth. But then I remembered a scene

171

in a movie where a girl with Tourette's syndrome screams, "Fuck balls!" So I guess it wasn't an original expression after all.

It is also very common for women to scream "holy fuck" during a wax. I'm not going to lie: when people start swearing and screaming, I often start laughing. I know that screaming and swearing makes them feel better, and it does not offend me one bit. But when one woman screamed "holy fuck," all I could think to say was, "I love when fucking becomes holy!" And I do.

15

Position #5: Swallowed by the Ass

A very plus-sized black lady came into the salon. She was wearing skinny jeans that were sagging all plumber-like around her hips. I could see her thong strings cutting into her sides above the waist of her pants. She had the sexiest and brightest six-inch heels on, and it was obvious that she sported a whole lot of sass. She was a beautiful woman with attitude, and I could tell it was going to be a fun experience. She had never been waxed before, but she told me that she heard I was the girl. Someone also told her that I did not care if she was a big girl, which is absolutely true, and that I was also the only girl in town who did not take close to an hour to do a Brazilian. Although it was obvious that she was very nervous about getting it done, I could tell that she was very excited as well. She was cooperative and flexible, and the waxing went very well. We chatted and laughed through the entire service. She was an absolute blast.

When she turned on her side, I did a pretty good job waxing her ass, even though it was hard to get at. I am proud to say that I have mastered getting into the dark, cavernous area that dwells between a person's cheeks no matter how far into the cave I have to dwell. But I have to admit that more than once I feared that I would get sucked into that dark cavern and never reappear. As I was imagining myself getting sucked in, she looked over her shoulder at me and said, "Now you can brag that you waxed the biggest ass in Rochester," to which I replied, "I've waxed bigger." So she said, "It must have been a black girl."

I hated to disappoint her, but I said, "She was white. And her ass was *so* big that I had to have her boyfriend spread her cheeks for me so I could even find my target."

We were both laughing so hard that I was afraid she was going to fall off the table. When she got up, she stood in front of the mirror, held her belly up to look at her lady parts, and said, "So that's what she looks like." Then she reached down, gave it a quick feel, and said, "It's so soft, I just want to touch it." And she did.

So it is true that I have had visions of getting sucked in by some of the bigger asses that I have waxed in my career. When the skin is dark and the ass is large, I have to work really hard to get to the promised land, and there have been times when I have envisioned getting sucked in and never resurfacing. It would be a strange way to die but, in my case, extremely fitting.

16

Long Live The Happy Hoo-Ha

Until I started writing my first book, I never realized how fun it would be to write about my work. Not only have I finished this one; I have notes and future illustrations started for one more. I think a trilogy, or maybe even a Happy Trail-ogy, would round out my storytelling and my career beautifully. And, if I play my cards right, maybe someday you will see me or even some of my work on television. Stranger things have happened.

So as I ventured through the Happy Hen House, I hope you agree that it is truly the place where every cock wants to go.

Made in the USA
Charleston, SC
16 May 2014